"Kristin Dempsey's workbook radiates hope for individuals grappling with su̲b̲s̲t̲a̲n̲c̲e̲ challenges. Through a compassionate harm reduction lens, this guide offers tangible strategies, inspiring not only recovery but also growth. Illuminating the path of self-discovery, it's a beacon of optimism and empowerment, essential for individuals and caregivers alike seeking a brighter, more fulfilling journey of healing."

> **—Christie Cline, MD, MBA**, CEO of ZiaPartners, Inc.; and past psychiatric medical director for the State of New Mexico Department of Health, Behavioral Health Services Division

"This book is an important addition to the growing literature on harm reduction-informed treatment. Following the principles, techniques, and spirit of motivational interviewing (MI), Dempsey helps people develop self-compassion, self-knowledge, and smart and clear goals to reduce drug-related harm. Numerous journal-like exercises help readers stay focused and build to a commitment to change—or not to."

> **—Patt Denning, PhD**, cofounder and former director of clinical services and training at the Harm Reduction Therapy Center; and coauthor of *Practicing Harm Reduction Psychotherapy*

"What a gem! Kristin Dempsey has served up a compassionate, safe, and thoughtful place for deeply exploring our relationship with substances—and ourselves. If you are someone who feels alone, doesn't like being told what to do, thinks about your own reasons and abilities for how you want to live your life, or if you simply relish the space and time to think for yourself, this is the resource for you!"

> **—Ali Hall, JD**, owner of Ali Hall Training and Consulting; member of the Motivational Interviewing Network of Trainers (MINT); and MINT-certified trainer

"*The Harm Reduction Workbook for Addiction* is a clearly written, eminently practical guide to help anyone struggling with substance use issues to find a starting place to make progress in change. It offers accessible 'self-help' tools in every chapter so that readers can work by themselves, or use the workbook as a supplement to more formal treatment. I highly recommend Dempsey's excellent work, whether for individuals or treatment providers."

—**Kenneth Minkoff, MD**, community and addiction psychiatrist; VP of ZiaPartners in Tucson, AZ; and international expert in integrated recovery-oriented services for people with co-occurring mental health and substance use disorders

"If you are wondering how to change your relationship with substances, this book is for you. This simple-to-follow guide invites you to explore and understand what works best for you, and supports you to decide when you are ready to do things differently. With the science of self-change, this book has a loving heart."

—**Glenn Hinds, BA(Hons), DipSW**, independent training consultant, counselor, and cohost of the *Talking To Change* podcast

"As someone dedicated to supporting recovery, I enthusiastically endorse Kristin Dempsey's *The Harm Reduction Workbook for Addiction*. This book is invaluable for individuals seeking recovery and clinicians searching for effective tools to guide their clients."

—**Suzzette Garcia**, licensed therapist, addiction counseling specialist, and past president of the California Association for Licensed Professional Clinical Counselors

"Change can be difficult, particularly when it comes to substance use. This workbook offers you a way forward that is personalized to your life, your experience, and your history. Rather than one-size-fits-all messaging or harsh judgments meant to shame you to change, you can apply this flexible and practical workbook to navigate the challenges you will encounter along your journey toward health and fulfillment."

—**Sebastian G. Kaplan, PhD**, associate professor at the Wake Forest University School of Medicine, cohost of the *Talking To Change* podcast, and coauthor of *Motivational Interviewing in Schools*

The *The* **Harm Reduction Workbook** *for* **Addiction**

Motivational Interviewing Skills to Create a Personalized Recovery Plan & Make Lasting Change

KRISTIN L. DEMPSEY, EDD, LMFT, LPCC

New Harbinger Publications, Inc.

NEW HARBINGER PUBLICATIONS is a registered trademark of New Harbinger Publications, Inc.

New Harbinger Publications is an employee-owned company.

Distributed in Canada by Raincoast Books

Copyright © 2024 by Kristin L. Dempsey
New Harbinger Publications, Inc.
5720 Shattuck Avenue
Oakland, CA 94609
www.newharbinger.com

Cover design by Amy Shoup

Acquired by Ryan Buresh

Edited by Jennifer Holder

All Rights Reserved

Library of Congress Cataloging-in-Publication Data on file

Printed in the United States of America

26   25   24

10   9   8   7   6   5   4   3   2   1   First Printing

Contents

Foreword

Books offering these tools of motivational interviewing or harm reduction are typically written for professionals and academics. In this workbook, Dr. Dempsey instead offers a way for anyone to examine their relationship to substances in a personal, intimate, and uniquely individual way, within the privacy of their own life.

As a longtime practitioner and trainer of motivational interviewing as well as an expert in harm reduction, I found this workbook exciting, entertaining, and completely accessible for anyone. It doesn't require us to go from chapter one to chapter two and so on. Rather, readers can view the topics of each chapter in the table of contents to see what "speaks" to them, and begin there. This workbook is grounded in personal choice, not another resource ready to tell you what you *should* do or think. I greatly appreciate this perspective, as will many readers.

The idea that we know best what we need to achieve our goals is at the center of this workbook. There are questions encouraging us to think about how we change, what motivates us to change, and when we might be ready to attempt a change. Through stories of others and their journeys of change—which are not provided to increase stigma or shame, or covertly inform us of the "right way" to make change—we connect to others as a reminder that rarely are we alone in wanting to make a change, especially in our relationship to substances. With worksheets that can be used over and over—and freely downloaded—we examine our desires, our strengths, our goals, and more, which helps readers view our relationship to substances with respect and clarity. Asking the reader to write how we feel or think about substances offers valuable tools in evaluating what we like about substances, as well as how we came to use them and why we might like to stop or cut down.

I particularly liked the section on self-compassion. After more than thirty-five years of working with thousands of patients and clients, I have found that few substance users who feel they are problematically or chaotically using a substance have much compassion for themselves, and certainly not for their use of substances. It is a sad commentary on our American culture that we have managed to stigmatize substances and those that use them at all. It means we begin to loathe ourselves, typically leading to *more* use of a substance to cope with that shame and guilt, not less. This lack of self-compassion then tends to restrict our ability to dispassionately view our use of substances and the relationship we now have with them. Using an onion as a metaphor, this book asks readers to consider how we can peel back the layers to understand our substance use. How are we ever to learn from our problematic use of substances, or work to improve our relationship to them? Without some self-compassion, why would we even try to change this relationship?

By encouraging our exploration of previous successes in other areas of our lives, we can link those successes to the possibility of improving our relationship to substances. This is a marvelous way to help us all see that changing our relationship to substances is possible, regardless of whether that change is moderation, abstinence, "sober curious," or something uniquely our own definition. With the acronym CLEAR, we consider: who can collaborate with us, what kind of time limits are reasonable to make this change; remember why we want to make this change or the emotional aspect of this change; the appreciable aspects of this change or small steps—what I call "baby steps"—we can take; and how we might refine this goal to remain flexible and possible. This reminds me of the greatest lesson the late G. Alan Marlatt taught me about change: that "we don't budget enough for change." While that is absolutely true, this workbook may just help tip the scale of our budgets over toward change!

After reading this workbook, I feel emboldened, empowered, and energized to tackle any change and thoroughly believe that you will too.

—Dee-Dee Stout, MA
Founding member of the Northern California
Association of Harm Reduction Therapists & Providers

Introduction

You likely opened this book because you have a relationship to substances, want to learn more about yourself, and are open to asking yourself some questions to see what you learn. Your curiosity is welcome. In these pages, you will have an opportunity to explore and decide what is most meaningful to you.

You are likely an inquisitive and determined person. Perhaps you have had some concerns about your use of substances or another problematic behavioral process, such as gambling. You wonder about your behaviors and are not sure what to make of them. But you want to know more about these substances in your life, you want to make choices, and you want a process that will work quickly and effectively. If you have attended or thought of attending a 12-step meeting, some sort of counseling, or even a treatment program, perhaps, for a whole number of reasons, these programs did not fit your needs. Whether you finished a program or not, you want more. You are quite possibly successful in many aspects of your life, and you want to explore your relation to substances—both the good things and the not so good things—effectively, confidentially, and quickly. Your seeking has led you here, and the exercises in this book have been designed to understand and maybe change your relationship with substances on your own terms, in a way that works for you.

This book provides guidance based on some of the best researched methods in substance-use recovery. As you explore your relationship with substances, some of the most useful and powerful ideas and tools developed will help you. This conversational workbook includes the philosophy of "harm reduction" and the practice of "motivational interviewing." Both help shape the exercises you are invited to do in each chapter.

About This Book

Harm reduction is an approach to managing substance use. It includes many ways to reduce, manage or stop substance use in order to prevent further harm from substance use while providing people with choice around which steps to take. As the Harm Reduction Therapy Center describes (2022), it is "based on the reality that behavior change is usually slow, and a leap from active substance use to complete abstinence is almost always unrealistic and often unnecessary to reduce or eliminate harm. Coercion and punishment are not helpful and, in fact, impede the process of true change." Essentially, any practices that help you cut back on using and that reduce self-harm are beneficial. Substance use itself is not a "good" or "bad" situation; there are always aspects of *both* benefit and harm related to use. True to the spirit of harm reduction, no specific outcome is expected as the result of working through this book. You might read this book and choose to move toward actively cutting back or discontinuing your substance use—or you may not. What is important is being open to explore change. As insights arise for you when I ask questions about your experiences, those insights and the responses you record in the writing exercises will be what open you up to change.

Motivational interviewing (MI) is an approach that provides a way to explore your questions and help guide you on a path toward change. MI is generally offered by practitioners to guide health seekers on journeys toward change. It has been tested in over two thousand controlled trials in various health care and social service industries. As an evidence-based process, it helps you start and focus your own exploration around what is and is not important to you, what kind of life you want, and the needs you have that will lead you to your best self. It can lead you to take the first steps in exploring your goals, which are about changing how you relate to and participate in substance use. In this workbook, the MI "conversations" happen on the page through writing exercises that encourage your reflections. As you learn about different ways of looking at substance use, you will also be invited to try on various lenses that may help you see yourself and your situation more clearly. My questions, or "prompts," and your written responses can therefore be seen as a kind of conversation.

These conversations about change happen through the "spirit" in which they occur and the skills you will explore. This "spirit" embraces the values and attitudes that will help you engage in conversations about change without judgment and shame, and with confidence and support. The skills help promote empathy and compassion toward yourself and your dilemma. Together, the spirit and the skills create a momentum toward change, while not asking or assuming you will change who you are and what you care about in life. Instead, you will engage in conversations about yourself, your dilemmas, and your values from a standpoint of curiosity and exploration. This book will not direct you into a path of action or toward obtaining a specific outcome. Based on who you are and what you want to bring with you on your journey, the skills and spirit of MI can be useful guides to help you move down a potential path of change. In this workbook, you will be on guided journey, with the structure of MI providing the tools you need to do the work you find meaningful and relevant for yourself.

Conversations about change will help you think about and understand what is important to you. This careful thought leads to productive action. Harm reduction provides a point of view that is curious and open to change, instead of being a set of strict rules and outcomes that you must follow in order to "get" the conversation about change "right." The potential to have a conversation about change without feeling pressured to come to a specific outcome can make you more likely to start that conversation. Motivational interviewing offers a method for *how* you can have these conversations about change. These communication skills have been proven for decades to start and extend conversations (Miller and Moyers 2021). Randee's story might give you an opportunity to see how such a conversation about change can happen.

★ Randee's Story

Randee is a thirty-two-year-old account executive. Since she was sixteen years old, she has been told she needs to "clean up her act." She binge drank through high school until she ended up in the emergency room with alcohol poisoning. Her fearful parents didn't know what to do. They reacted by insisting that sixteen-year-old Randee go to a residential rehabilitation center. The rehab program incorporated a 12-step model with some cognitive behavioral interventions to help Randee manage urges to use. Randee was both angry and scared—and a thousand miles away from home. She often felt unsafe telling counselors what she really thought about her program and recovery, because she did not want to be dropped into a lower "phase" or leave the program. Not wanting to rock the boat anymore with her parents and feeling terribly homesick, Randee complied with program rules and activities, although she never felt being "clean and sober" was her choice. Recovery was defined for her, and she had no ability to question the process or explore her own reasons for change. She did, however, spend at least half an hour a day journaling about the negative impact of her use and her character defects that brought her to problematic alcohol use.

Sixteen years later, Randee feels confused and unsure about her relationship to alcohol. After the program, she remained abstinent from alcohol for sixteen months, but she started to use alcohol again when she went to college. She was able to avoid binge drinking, but she has been habitually using alcohol. Lately, Randee notices that she is both drinking more alcohol and drinking more frequently throughout the week. She is experiencing more hangovers, and is concerned that she feels more agitated when she does not have an opportunity to drink.

She wants to change her relationship with alcohol, but she does not necessarily want to quit. Randee knows she does not want to attend group meetings or go through a program. She would like to have an opportunity to explore her drinking habits privately and on her own time. Randee just wants to understand herself better, and she wants a place to start. She is attracted to this workbook, as she wants to be able to journal and understand herself without feeling like she has to say certain things in order to be "right." She values having a guide that helps her sort out her own feelings and goals, and that assists her in creating a clear path to understanding her relationship with alcohol.

How to Use This Workbook

Like Randee, you may want guidance without lecture, and an opportunity to explore your own reasons for change in privacy and at your own pace. This book starts with an exploration of the motivational interviewing process. You will learn how to engage in the "spirit" of MI, using specific interaction techniques on yourself to explore and refine your own change plan, which is made up of your personal steps toward the goals of your choice. You will learn to identify your own change language as it occurs and take steps to build an initial pathway to your desired goal.

As you read the book, you'll have opportunities to reflect and answer questions about yourself and your experiences and to complete helpful exercises and worksheets. Many of the exercises and worksheets are available for download at the website for this book: http://www.newharbinger. com/51901. For more details on this, see the very back of this book.

While it's recommended that you complete the exercises in each chapter sequentially, you can move around the workbook and complete the exercises that are the most relevant to you. Not sure where to start? Check out the content of the chapters and begin engaging with the topics that are most meaningful to you:

- Want to engage in a conversation about change with yourself? Start with chapter 1.

- If self-judgment and lack of worth is a particular concern for you, check out chapter 2.

- Being able to grow as you change requires openness, willingness to reach out to others for help, and connection to our own self-compassion. If these issues are of particular interest, go to chapter 3.

- A crucial part of doing something different with your life is figuring out what is important to you so you have fuel available that promotes change. Chapter 4 discusses discovering personal meaning and ways you can connect with your own personal power to promote change.

- Ready to listen to your change? Then you might like to start with chapter 5 on self-reflection.

- If you notice that you are hard on yourself and cannot identify your strengths and places of potential growth, explore chapter 6 on affirmation.

- It takes a village to help change along. Chapter 7 will address how to gather support from others to promote change.

- Growth is promoted by your ability to ask yourself some challenging questions that can evoke important reasons, needs, and desires to change your current relationship with substances. Ready to start asking yourself these questions? Start with chapter 8.

- Get ready, set, and focus on change. Chapter 9 is how you move to focus your efforts and prepare to make the next move toward change.

- Chapter 10 is your guide to moving from where you are now to your next action step. Your step might be small, or it might be larger, but it will be defined and shaped by your needs, abilities, and resources. Chapter 10 will be most helpful after you complete enough chapters to gain the insight you need to make the first move.

Welcome to a conversational journey! This book can lead you to rewarding, exciting, thoughtful growth opportunities. I admire your willingness to take the first steps.

CHAPTER 1

Engage a Conversation with Yourself

You are now thinking about taking the next step to look at how you are relating to substances. It is helpful to start by asking yourself some questions that will help you gain more self-understanding. In this chapter, you are invited to explore what is important to you, especially what you care about and what you might want to change in your life. Deanne's story offers a place to get started. Her concerns and challenges may help you see how a conversation with yourself can open you up to new ideas and paths toward change.

★ Deanne's Story

Deanne started drinking alcohol and occasionally using cannabis in high school. She fondly remembers the parties and concerts where she drank as her favorite times. Deanne is now twenty-eight, and she questions where her life is going. She wonders in particular if drinking and cannabis use are helping her or setting her back. She still likes to drink now and again, and spend time with friends at clubs. She also notices that she is getting bored, and questions if she wants to do other things with her life. She might go to college or maybe pursue a committed relationship and start a family. She is not sure what she wants to do next. What she *is* sure of is that she is spending more time weekly, and sometimes daily, drinking or smoking. She wonders if she is holding herself back.

The Substance-Use Continuum

You may not be quite sure if you have a problem with substances, or whether you are an *addict* or a *problem user* or *drinker*. Such terms are loaded and often carry significant judgments. They come with various negative images about what it means to have a problem. A challenge with this thinking is the idea that one either *has* or *does not have* a problem. The reality is that we are located along a continuum of substance use and abuse, the nature of which is commonly observed in treatment programs and is currently a target for further study (National Institute on Alcohol Abuse and Alcoholism 2020). Here is a sense of the continuum:

- When we start to use substances, often (but not always) in adolescence, we might just try out or "dabble" in alcohol or other drugs.

- As teens or young adults, we may start to have more regular but nonproblematic use, and this type of use is known as "social drinking" or "social using."

- When we start to drink regularly without consequences—which are unwanted, unhelpful, and unintended results of using substances—we might be engaging in more "habitual patterns."

- Before mental health professionals identify a "substance use disorder," they assess our behavior, such as being intoxicated or withdrawing from use of a substance. If our particular combination of behavioral, cognitive, emotional, and even potential physical conditions is significantly impacting our life—as the direct result of using the identified substance—we may have a substance use disorder (American Psychiatric Association 2022).

With these definitions, you might see where you are located on this continuum. As you move farther along the continuum from experimenting to abuse, the substances you use gain increasing control of your life.

Circle where you might be located along the continuum.

I am dabbling or experimenting.

I'm drinking or using socially.

I use as part of a habitual pattern.

The effects on my life indicate I might have substance use disorder.

The good news is that if you locate yourself on the continuum, you can make choices now that can help you avoid being at the far end of the continuum, at "dependence," where you might experience both physical as well as psychological need for a substance.

Your Obstacles to Facing Substance Use

It is tempting to turn away and keep on using. Here are some reasons you might hide from conversations with yourself or others about substance use.

You Feel Alone

As you question your relationship with substances, you might feel alone. But you are *not* alone.

- According to a 2019 national survey, 85.6 percent of people over the age of eighteen indicated they drank at some point in their lives, with almost 55 percent reporting they drank in the last month (National Institute on Alcohol Abuse and Alcoholism 2022).

- Of those who use alcohol, over 25 percent stated they participated in binge use of alcohol; binge use is typically defined as five drinks for men and four drinks for women on the same occasion.

- A little over 9 percent of the US adult population uses "any illicit" drug, with cannabis still being included in the definition of illicit drug in 2019. Although this appears to be a small number, it adds up to over 29 million people.

You might feel lonely in your relationship with substances, but you are hardly alone.

You Resist Support from Others

You might assume that if someone has a problem with substances, they must go to a treatment center, therapist, or 12-step group for treatment or community help. Although such support can be incredibly helpful and is highly recommended, the reality is that only about 10 percent of people with substance use disorders receive treatment (National Institute on Alcohol Abuse and Alcoholism 2019). This reveals a sad reality—that there is a lack of access to treatment programming, which might also be a reason you are reading this book. Yet, if you are at the "dabbling" or "social" levels on the continuum of use, you might very well change your substance use significantly by using the self-exploration resources in this book. If you are in the "habitual pattern" or "substance use disorder" levels on the continuum, you might learn more about the substance use, and what you learn can help provide insight into your next steps toward treatment or self-help support.

You Don't Want to Be Told What to Do

It is possible that you are someone who does not want to be told what to do. Maybe a number of people are pestering you about your relationship with a substance, which has made it hard to open up to the possibility of change. Your reaction to being pestered is completely normal. In fact, some evolutionary psychologists think that humans have learned to push back or resist unwanted advice from others to avoid being too submissive in our social groups, which reduces our power in the social hierarchy. Although social dominance might have contributed to human evolutionary success, we tend to want to avoid being told which roles we will take on and who will have authority over us (de Almeida Neto 2017). Even though you are reading this book in the twenty-first century, at times your subcortical brain is thinking for you—as if it were over five thousand years ago! So, maybe it's not a great idea for anyone to start barking orders about what you should and should not do. Rest assured, this book offers you a way to explore some of your ideas at your own pace and in your own time so you can come to your own conclusions. Here is how Deanne experienced resistance to facing her substance use:

> Deanne is aware that she can be hard on herself. She notices thoughts about how she is a "loser" and that she "doesn't deserve" to have the things she wants because she has wasted so much time not doing things she cares about, such as traveling with friends and finishing a college program. She also doesn't want to hear others' opinions about her use. In the last couple of years, her mom, sister, and best friend have all made comments about her drinking and cannabis use. At first, she cut back a lot, as she was ashamed that she might be out of control. Cutting back lasted a few months, but Deanne noticed that she started to move back to drinking and using some cannabis on the weekends. Gradually, she started using during the week as well.

Write about your resistance to facing substance use. Why might it feel hard to look at this?

_____

_____

_____

_____

_____

_____

Overcome the Waiting Game

As you explore your relationship with substances, you may feel confused and alone. Because of the shame and stigma associated with using substances, you might have waited a long time, sometimes a very long time, to take a step toward change. Waiting is a problem because the longer you wait, the more likely you will lose things you care about—relationships, money, career, and self-respect. You might feel trapped in an unfair and unavoidable situation. The thinking goes like this: *My shame and self-consciousness keep me from asking for help, yet I also have no idea what to do next. As time goes on, my situation with substances or other potentially problematic behavior is not improving.*

It is completely understandable how you or anyone in such a situation might feel overwhelmed, scared, and even hopeless. This is where motivational interviewing can provide the hope you so desperately need. The approach values your curiosity and willingness to explore through conversations with yourself. This can help open the door to ideas and possibilities that you may not have considered yet.

> Deanne opened this book because she wanted some answers, and most importantly, she wanted some direction toward change. Although she is not exactly sure if she would choose cutting down or quitting entirely, she wants a place to start. A friend invited her to attend a 12-step meeting with him, but she finds going to meetings terrifying. She is concerned that someone she knows will be there, and she doesn't want coworkers to hear gossip about her. But she wants to start somewhere, and this book gives her a place to take her first steps.

How are you feeling as you begin this conversation with yourself?

_____

_____

_____

What thoughts are currently running through your mind?

_____

_____

_____

_____

It is important to verbalize the dilemmas you are struggling to change. Thoughts might only be thoughts, but in our heads, they contain a lot of power. They are not always helpful, especially when they contribute to rumination and remaining stuck. Speaking out loud about your dilemmas draws attention to the *content* of your thoughts. You can then better hear what is in your head. Try this out yourself.

Notice one thought you are having right now about your relationship to substances, and write one to two sentences about it:

_____

_____

_____

_____

_____

Now read your statement out loud. Notice if the content feels different when you can *hear* your words instead of *think* your words.

Deanne thought about her relationship to alcohol and cannabis. She found herself talking out loud about being able to "take or leave" cannabis, but she also noticed that she speaks about alcohol like a buddy she has relied on for a long time, for comfort and support. She was surprised to notice herself saying these words and having such feelings about alcohol.

We're going to explore your motivation for starting to change your behavior around substances throughout this book. For now, consider how stating your intention to change out loud, to someone else, might feel different than only thinking it in your own mind. What are the effects of speaking to another person of your intention to change? What might happen?

_____

_____

_____

_____

_____

_____

One common response is that speaking to another person, or speaking to ourselves through writing, causes more thoughts about change to arise. Exploring your reasons for change has the potential to churn up change-oriented thoughts, feelings, and potential behaviors. Whenever you are involved in a dilemma of any kind, you'll find that a lot of internal dialogue and emotions arise. When you explore those experiences, you'll find it makes perfect sense that such exploration has the potential to churn up more reasons, needs, desires, and movements toward change.

Consider talk about change, or "change talk" as we will call it in this book, as the entry portal to the potential for change. The exploring process is taking the stairs down into the dilemma. A thorough exploration is a curious search of all the motivational nooks and crannies that exist inside you. In this way, your exploring and dropping into your dilemma is how you start to move the logjam of stuckness.

Gain Clarity on Your Attitude

Have you tried quitting substances before you opened this book? It is quite likely that you have. It is common for us to try a number of times to quit or cut back on substances before we make any significant changes in our use pattern. There are many reasons why cutting back or quitting is so difficult: withdrawals are uncomfortable, it is hard to give up what might have been (at least sometimes) an enjoyable lifestyle, or substance use can function as a coping mechanism that helps us deal with a number of challenging life situations. The emotional, physical, and behavioral challenges associated with quitting a substance are many, and often we quit when we are compelled to do so by external factors, such as a partner threatening to leave, or internal factors, such as illness or injury.

Just considering these challenges can discourage us from quitting or cutting back, and, ironically, it's here that we can begin exploring the ingredients that help us prepare for change. One of the most important places to start is looking at our own attitudes about ourselves and what we do and do not deserve in terms of recovery and healing.

You might have heard someone say, "If change were so easy, we would have done it already," and there is truth to that. "Just Do It" might be a memorable slogan for an athletic company marketing to the sometimes-motivated athlete, but it doesn't work when it comes to addiction. Our combination of emotional and biological experiences that reinforce staying the same can be very difficult to overcome.

So, if changing behavior is so difficult, where does that leave you? This book walks you through activities that build momentum toward change. Our attitude can move us toward change or keep us stuck in how we are today. An *attitude* is how we think about something, and it is often influenced by our values. Your attitudes also increase your motivation toward change or hold you back from change.

If you think about your attitudes toward substance use, what words come to mind? Here are some examples of common attitudes (Spacey 2021, January 12). Circle the attitudes that feel most compelling to you:

Accept	Confident	Enterprising	Objective	Serious
Active	Conservative	Enthusiastic	Obnoxious	Sincere
Adverse	Considerate	Festive	Open	Skeptical
Aggressive	Contemptuous	Flexible	Opinionated	Snobby
Agreeable	Cooperative	Forgiving	Optimistic	Somber
Aloof	Courageous	Fragile	Outgoing	Strong
Ambitious	Courteous	Friendly	Overconfident	Stubborn
Amenable	Critical	Giving	Passionate	Sympathetic
Animated	Curious	Gloomy	Passive	Thoughtful
Anxious	Cynical	Glum	Patient	Timid
Apathetic	Daring	Good	Patronizing	Tireless
Approachable	Dark	Grounded	Pessimistic	Tolerant
Assertive	Decisive	Hesitant	Pleasant	Trusting
Authoritative	Defeatist	Hopeful	Polite	Unaffected
Bad	Dejected	Hostile	Poor	Unapproachable
Biased	Dependent	Humble	Positive	Unassuming
Bold	Determined	Impartial	Practical	Unbiased
Brave	Devoted	Impatient	Professional	Uncommunicative
Buoyant	Diligent	Impolite	Rational	Understanding
Callous	Disagreeable	Inflexible	Realistic	Unenthusiastic
Calm	Disengaged	Inhospitable	Reasonable	Unfriendly
Candid	Disgruntled	Interested	Reliable	Unpretentious
Carefree	Disgusted	Intolerant	Reluctant	Unprofessional
Careful	Disinterested	Irresponsible	Remote	Unrealistic
Careless	Dismissive	Joyous	Resentful	Unwavering
Caring	Disrespectful	Liberal	Reserved	Unwelcoming
Cautious	Distant	Lighthearted	Resilient	Warm
Cheerful	Distrustful	Lively	Respectful	Weak
Cold	Emotional	Miserable	Responsible	Willing
Commanding	Empathetic	Motivated	Responsive	Withdrawn
Committed	Energetic	Negative	Selfish	
Condescending	Engaged	Neutral	Selfless	

Look at the attitudes you circled. Which ones might allow you to be more open to exploring your relationship to substance use?

_____

_____

_____

Which ones close you down or cut you off from doing such exploration?

_____

_____

_____

The good news about your attitudes is that they change based on your situation. They are not a fixed part of your personality. You might, for example, be more closed off and unfriendly around people you do not know, but more open and talkative when you feel comfortable and safe around friends. Because attitudes are not fixed, you can change your attitude toward anything as long as you are aware of your attitude.

The Spirit of This Workbook

The "spirit of motivational interviewing" is the phrase used to describe the attitudes and values promoted by practitioners who use MI to support their clients (Miller and Rollnick 2023. The "spirit" of MI is likely the most important part of helping people change, because the practitioner's attitudes and values create psychological safety in the conversation about change. You will find that spirit guiding you throughout this workbook.

Generally, when someone feels that they are not going to be judged or bossed around and that they have control over their decisions, they are more likely to start a conversation about things that are important to them. Deanne's story gives us an example of how impactful attitude can be in shifting behavior.

Deanne was not sure about whether she had what it takes to quit using cannabis or alcohol. She had been smoking since she was fourteen, and now she is forty-two. She had become so used to being told why she should "just quit" that she avoided talking about her smoking or drinking at all. Yet inside, Deanne felt a strong urge to take the first steps to quit or cut back on her cannabis or alcohol use. She knew it would be hard, and she knew she needed help. She just could not face another judgmental comment or unaccepting look. Quitting cannabis and alcohol is hard enough, and, because of people's attitudes, she felt it simply was not worth taking the risk of speaking to someone about her dilemma.

Think about what is on the line for Deanne. She tells herself she might want to just quit. It makes sense that she would want some support, as we know that quitting is so difficult, and it is made even more difficult by holding it all inside. Yet, here she is avoiding a conversation with anyone who might help because she is so reactive to judgment. Keeping things as they are—continuing to smoke and drink—is the default, despite the potentially negative consequences for her. Deanne's dilemma is one of the consequences of having experienced unwelcoming or judgmental attitudes about substance use—attitudes that often are held even by people who want to be helpful!

Consider yourself for a moment. When did you avoid asking for help or talking about a challenge in your life because you did not feel emotionally safe? Describe a time when you did not want to be hassled, judged, or lectured to by someone:

_____

_____

_____

_____

_____

_____

_____

_____

Looking at what you wrote, what would you have needed to be different for you to feel more open to talking with someone? Write down what you need to feel psychologically safe:

_____

_____

_____

_____

_____

_____

_____

Core Values of Motivational Interviewing

In the preceding section, it is likely that you wrote down some ideas that are very much part of the spirit of MI, such as acceptance, empowerment, partnership, and compassion. In this workbook, you will apply the spirit of MI to approach your change process with openness and curiosity in order to create psychological safety. If you cannot feel safe, you will not take risks to explore your substance or process-related problems. It is also important to be clear about what the spirit of MI is *not*: it does not involve spirituality or religion. Although spirituality or religion can be part of your recovery, this is a secular approach to exploring your relationship to substance use.

When engaging in this conversation about change, you are *doing* something—using specific techniques or engaging in various exercises. In addition, the way you are, your *being*—that is your values, attitudes, and all the ways you show up for the conversation—is just as important, if not more important than the skills you use. This is because your values provide direction for your change. How you move toward those values can change over time. There is no single right way to move toward what you care about in this process. However, *not* knowing what you care about creates a difficult situation because not knowing your values is a bit like trying to find an address without a map or GPS.

In the upcoming chapters, you will explore values to learn about your relationship to substance use in ways that promote both safety and awareness. When you can connect to your values, you will truly embody their healing potential. Think about this as the foundation of openness and safety that allows for the rest of your recovery house to be built. In the next chapter, you will explore acceptance. Openness to your own experience and reality is a key component to understanding your relationship to unhelpful substances or processes in your life. First, however, let's explore change a bit more.

Your Own Reasons for Change

Exploring and eliciting *your own reasons for change* is a critical component of change conversations. You may notice that care providers who collaborate with you—whether a family member, a spouse, or even a therapist in a health care or human services setting—stir feelings of resistance within you. Many of us can relate to the problem of being told what to do or advised in a particular way that leaves out our own choices or control agency in the matter. By ignoring personal choice and reasons for change, these care providers may unintentionally trigger your resistance. Motivational interviewing has a specific understanding of resistance: it happens when you are out of sync with someone, and they do not provide you with choice regarding your own change process (Miller and Rollnick 2023). By starting with your own reasons for change, you will experience reduced resistance as you explore your own needs and wants.

Ironically, you may have created your own resistance when you think about all the reasons that others want you to make a change and then you try to conform to their wishes. In some cases, especially when the stakes are high (for example, losing a friendship, creating conflict in a marriage, being disciplined on a job), you might make the change. However, many of us resist. That resistance shows up consciously or unconsciously as refusing to participate in exploring the change process. Consider your own experience with substances in the following exercise.

My Own Reasons for Change

First, list what others tell you they would like you to change and what you think about the change goals that others have for you. Then write down what you do in response to the change goals that others have for you. Finally, list your own reason for change. After completing the table, answer the questions to help you consider the impact of exploring your own reasons for change.

What others want me to change	What I think about others' change goals for me	What I do in response others' change goals for me	My own reason for change
Example: Stop smoking cannabis.	I have enjoyed cannabis. I have found it has helped me through the hardest times.	I avoid talking to family members who bring up my smoking. I avoid family get-togethers where the issue might come up.	I want to explore how I am impacted by cannabis. I will consider cutting back if it seems to be beneficial for me.

Explore your own reason for change compared to what others think.

On a scale of 1 to 10, where 1 is not important and 10 is extremely important, _____ how important is it for you to do what others want you to do?

How important is it for you to do what you want to do?   _____

Notice the difference in the numbers. What comes up for you in terms of your interest and desire to change? Do any emotions arise? Write about the feelings.

_____

_____

_____

_____

It is likely you are more motivated to move toward your *own* goals instead of the goals others set for you. This was the case for Deanne.

Deanne definitely noticed how her goals differed from the goals of her family and friends. She was able to write about how the most important people in her life made their desire for her to quit using alcohol very clear to her. She became aware of her own defensive reactions over the last several years when they brought up some of her behaviors, such as missing work, getting into arguments, and spending too much money and time in bars. Deanne also noticed that it was painful to think about the various confrontations over time, and she welcomed the chance to focus on her own thoughts about where she would like to address her concerns with alcohol.

She thought carefully about the question and decided that she wanted to have an opportunity to learn more about how alcohol might be impacting her desire to do more with her life. She thought about the hard decisions she might have to make regarding whether she should quit or cut back. Deanne found that creating this starting goal for herself gave her some comfort, and thought she might have what she needs to start learning about herself. Although exploring how alcohol might impact her life is a small goal, it felt like a safe place to start, and Deanne was open to exploring this topic further.

What's Next

Now that you have started the conversation with yourself and considered some of your reasons for exploring and desire to change, you will now move a bit deeper. You may be wondering what change might mean for you and how you might start such a change process. In chapter 2, you will explore further how acceptance of your situation and of yourself can help you get out of your own way as you move toward change.

Drop Judgment and Embrace Acceptance

Acceptance has long been a part of substance use recovery. When questioning your relationship to substances, acceptance is a helpful first step. This is because using substances is a behavior typically coupled with shame and regret in many cultures. Shame may keep you out of treatment, interfere with current treatment, and can cause relapse. It is also why the Serenity Prayer, a powerful statement of acceptance and letting go of control, is typically always shared at 12-step meetings.

> God, grant me the serenity to accept the things I cannot change, the courage to change the things I can, and the wisdom to know the difference.

Written in 1937 by Reinhold Niebuhr (Sifton, 2003), this version of the Serenity Prayer is known widely and held closely by those who find comfort in its wisdom: knowing when to let go and when to actively pursue change. The ability to step back and be open to what can and cannot be changed is a critical component of letting go of trying to control the people, places, and things that trigger urges to use.

Acceptance does not mean that you approve of or enjoy a situation—it simply means you are not denying the reality of a situation. When you stop fighting against what is and stop pining for what you wish were the situation, you can relate to reality more effectively (Linehan 2014). Acceptance allows you to be open to the hand that has been dealt. Knowing your hand as it is in the present moment allows you to decide how you will play that hand. Acceptance frees you up to make the most effective and meaningful next move.

In motivational interviewing, acceptance has four specific components known as "the four As": absolute worth, affirmation, accurate empathy, and autonomy (Miller and Rollnick 2023). Each of these components of acceptance provides a specific way in which we can step back from judgment and control to move toward openness and understanding. We need to be reminded frequently of acceptance so we can repeatedly refocus on being open to reality and to move away from shame and regret. We will explore each of its components as we move through this chapter. Let's look at acceptance more closely.

Your Perception of How Things Are

Acceptance is your ability to honor the current reality of the situation and to participate in it without judgment and without resisting what is. For example, if I accept my substance use as it is occurring right now, I am more able to notice how I am experiencing this reality. I might notice that when I think about how often I use alcohol, I feel a pit in my stomach. Perhaps I am aware of telling myself that I am a "loser" whenever I think of how much cannabis I smoke each day. Accepting reality does not mean that you like reality (Linehan 1993). Instead, accepting reality means that you are now open to moving away from denial and making it seem less impactful than it is, and also moving away from other unhelpful defenses that can keep you stuck. Once you have this openness and can experience your reality and describe it, you become able to make choices regarding how to respond to it. In chapter 1, we began following Deanne's story. Let's look now at her relationship to acceptance.

★ Deanne's Story

Deanne noticed that she often tells herself that she doesn't have what it takes to be a success because she has spent so much time drinking instead of "doing something" with her life. When she paused to observe how harshly she evaluates herself, she was able to step back and see that she has these thoughts that she should not be a success, but she has no evidence that supports such thoughts. In fact, she is able to list various accomplishments she has achieved in her work as a veterinary assistant. Even though she looks forward to potentially making a career change down the road, she was able to think about the various training and certifications she received in order to do her work well. She also thought about ways in which she had supported pet owners during very trying times as they dealt with their pet's serious illness or death. Deanne sometimes found that providing such emotional support was difficult, but she remained proud that she was able to deal with some very challenging emotional issues and situations.

Moving from nonacceptance to acceptance can seem tricky. If you tell yourself "just accept it," that approach is not likely to be effective. After all, we tell ourselves to "just do" things all the time, and these are not usually helpful demands. The path to moving from nonacceptance or judging yourself to accepting yourself is found in your ability to notice and replace judgmental words with descriptions of what you are noticing. The judgment links to your view of the situation, which might be distorted. For example, consider this statement: "I am such a loser because I get so emotional when my family starts drinking over the holidays and I am not mature enough to handle it." Now, imagine this statement rewritten as a description without judgmental language: "I notice that I feel sad and angry when my family members start to drink a lot of wine over the holidays because I am worried we will start fighting." Can you see and feel the difference between these two statements? It is likely you notice the second statement is not about the individual taking blaming or labeling themself. It is difficult to get beyond the judgment in the first statement, as it feels like it's all about individual defects. With the second descriptive statement, the reason the person feels upset makes sense given the situation. You might be able to imagine how they eventually could make some choices that would help them manage their fear and sadness.

Try noticing your own judgmental statements about your substance use and replace them with descriptions about yourself instead. This exercise is an opportunity for practicing suspending judgment and moving toward accepting reality, something that you will work on throughout this book. This exercise is available for download at http://www.newharbinger.com/51901.

Learning to Notice Instead of Judge

Observe your thoughts for a day and watch for examples of self-judgment. Write those judgments in the first column of the table, and then look at them in light of the subsequent columns. Use the example in the first row as a guide.

As you fill in the columns in the table, ask yourself, *How can I start* noticing *instead of* judging *myself?*

My own judgment	How this judgment makes me feel and think	Shifting from judging to noticing	How noticing what's happening makes me feel and think
Example: I should be smoking less weed. I am a loser.	Hopeless. Why try? I am annoyed with myself.	I notice that when I smoke throughout the day, I do not complete all the chores I was hoping to finish.	I feel curious about what might happen if I finish my chores before smoking.

As Deanne practiced noticing rather than judging, she realized she sometimes tells herself she is unworthy of love and attention from anyone who might be a promising intimate partner. She reviewed various relationships in her past and noticed how she often let others take advantage of her time and money because she did not think she really deserved to be treated any differently. When she identified some automatic judgmental messages, she was able to ask herself, *What have I done to really deserve this thought about myself?* She could not answer that question.

Although Deanne did not immediately adopt a different perspective about herself, asking this question made her original automatic thought around being unlovable and unworthy less impactful. She could tell that she was being hard on herself.

You might be similar to Deanne regarding some of your own self-judgments. It is also quite possible that you have a very different concern.

What did you learn from completing the "Learning to Notice Instead of Judge" exercise? Did you notice a shift, even a small one, in how you are thinking about yourself, your life situation, and others? Spend some time rereading each judging and noticing statement, pausing for a few moments between each statement. Just notice what thoughts are emerging and what feelings you might experience in your body. Write here what you are thinking and feeling as you sit with the judging and noticing statements:

_____

_____

_____

_____

_____

_____

Overcoming Shame and Regret

We are working to build a compassionate foundation for your substance use exploration that helps you stand strong against shame and regret. Each of the following exercises will move you through the components ("the 4 As") of acceptance—absolute worth, affirmation, autonomy, and accurate empathy—and will help guide your openness to further exploration of your substance use.

Absolute Worth

Judging ourselves is part of the human condition. When substance use enters the equation, judgment of self and others is almost universal. Much of this has to do with the way substance use causes us to behave or appear to others. Consider the jokes and images that come to mind when considering the host of sitcoms, movies, comic routines, and social media posts featuring intoxicated individuals. It is easy to remember the characters played by W. C. Fields and Dean Martin as acting ridiculous; we also remember the tragic characters, such as Joe and Kirsten in *Days of Wine and Roses* or Don Birnam in *The Lost Weekend*. Such characters and stories are just a tiny sample of cultural messages that we receive about the humiliating and undesirable effects of substance use.

Yet, most of us use at least one substance, and over half of us use drugs—including nicotine—in ways that can be considered abusive (National Center for Drug Abuse Statistics 2022). Most of us engage in behavior that we likely feel self-conscious about or might question, but the impact of our behavior is hard to openly explore when we feel judged by others or ourselves.

Exploring Self-Judgment and Absolute Worth

You can work with your worthiness as a person (absolute worth) as you notice judgments about your substance use. Write an example of a self-judgment about your substance use at the top of the worksheet. Then notice and record what feelings come up when you think about that judgment. If you do not have a feeling word, notice what comes up in your body. Record this feeling or sensation at the top of the sheet.

Next, turn to the following chart, which will help you consider alternatives when the self-judgment comes up. In the first column, describe other behaviors you were involved in that day. It could be taking kids to school, making sure you eat breakfast, saying "hi" to a neighbor. It can be a large or small behavior. What strengths, related to that behavior, do you notice during the day? (If you need help, check out the list of strengths in chapter 6).

In the second column, make a statement about your own self-worth as you notice your own strengths. Then, in the last column, indicate how you feel after making your self-worth statement. If you struggle to put words to feelings, this online list can help you express emotions: http://www.psychpage .com/learning/library/assess/feelings.html.

Here's a worksheet example to get you started.

One way I judge myself about substance use is: I am outright sloppy when I drink.

The feeling or sensation of this judgment is: Embarrassment

Description of other behavior I was involved in today	Strength word (as it relates to your behavior)	Self-worth statement	Feeling or sensation of strength and self-worth
I have not used this week, and I successfully collaborated on a project with my team at work.	Reliable	I show up for others.	Confidence.

Now it's your turn. You can download this worksheet at http://www.newharbinger.com/51901 to fill it out as many times as you like.

One way I judge myself about substance use is: _____

The feeling or sensation of this judgment is: _____

Description of other behavior I was involved in today	Strength word (as it relates to your behavior)	Self-worth statement	Feeling or sensation of strength and self-worth

Affirming your absolute worth can help you explore and consider change because it can help you understand that you deserve to grow. Growth and change can be seen as a right every person can enjoy. No matter what might have occurred in your past, you deserve the opportunity to build the future.

Affirmation

Many of us consider affirmation as the way we cheerlead or support one another, such as saying, "You can do this." I have worked with counselors who had affirmations taped to their desks: "All I need is within me right now" or "I am constantly growing and evolving into a better person." Such statements can be helpful coping tools, but motivational interviewing takes a different spin on what it means to affirm someone. The spirit of MI promotes the willingness to notice and speak to our strengths, instead of immediately working to change or "fix" others or ourselves (Miller and Rollnick 2023). What strengths do you notice, and want to affirm?

Affirming My Strengths

By affirming what is right with us, we can accept our whole self, including the parts that are struggling. List five of your strengths to which you can immediately connect at this moment. If you have difficulty with this, check out the list of strengths in chapter 6. To feel the effect of affirmation, write examples of when you exercised each strength. You can download this worksheet at http://www.newharbinger.com/51901.

Strength	Example of When I Demonstrated This Strength
Example: Determination	I got my degree, even though I had to work full time during my entire college career.
Example: Friendliness	I am the person at work everyone feels comfortable talking to when we socialize during breaks and after work.

Consider how your strengths can support your exploration of your use of substances. Write three strengths that are helping you as you interact with this workbook.

1. _____

2. _____

3. _____

Affirming your strength helps you take a different view of your challenges. Seeing what is "strong with you instead of what is wrong with you" helps you own that change is possible. It is difficult for anyone to feel as if they can be a different person if they only focus on their problems. Knowing your concerns is good as a place to get started, and knowing your strengths is important for moving forward.

Accurate Empathy

To successfully have conversations about change, we need to feel heard and accepted for who we are. We need those listening to accurately reflect what we say. *Accurate empathy* is a term used to describe what happens when someone is able to correctly understand and states back to another person how they are feeling. This is not telling someone how they feel, but mirroring back the emotional component of a person's words as well as their facial and body communication (Miller and Rollnick 2023). When I feel someone "gets" me, I know I am accepted, and I will continue to explore my thoughts and feelings.

Consider your acceptance of yourself. Is there a way for you to explore your own thoughts and feelings in order to be empathetic toward yourself? Can you accurately identify and label your emotions? The answers to these questions are important, because your ability to notice and then label how you feel increases self-compassion. It helps you consider how to respond to a problem instead of automatically reacting to it or avoiding it. This is what having accurate empathy toward yourself accomplishes.

Exploring Accurate Empathy for Yourself

As you begin this exercise, practice noticing and labeling your emotions. First, identify an uncomfortable situation you were in because of your substance use. Then fill in the rest of the worksheet. Here's an example.

Uncomfortable situation because of my substance use: I was out of control at our holiday office party.

My immediate thoughts and feelings	Feelings and sensations	What did this mean to me?	"I feel _____ because _____."
I drank way too much, and my coworkers probably think I'm a clown.	Sadness Embarrassment Tight stomach Nausea	I don't want to feel disrespected. I am worried others think less of me.	I feel ashamed because I behaved in an undignified way around my colleagues.

Now it's your turn. You can download this worksheet at http://www.newharbinger.com/51901 to use as many times as you like.

Uncomfortable situation due to my substance use: _____

My immediate thoughts and feelings	Feelings and sensations	What did this mean to me?	"I feel _____ because _____ ."

In the final column, you completed a reflective listening statement. Reread the statement. After reading it again, write what else you would like to say about your substance use.

_____

_____

_____

_____

_____

_____

Did you find yourself elaborating on what you were thinking about the difficult situation? Accurate empathy helps us do that. Noticing your own accurate empathy toward yourself can help deepen your self-understanding, which in turn can help you articulate the language of change needed to take the next step in changing your substance use behaviors.

Autonomy

The fourth component of acceptance is your autonomy—that is, your individual choices and attempts at making your own decisions. Autonomy relates to acceptance, because to be truly accepting of anyone, we cannot be invested in controlling their choices. Consider your relationship to substances. Have you had an experience in which someone, who may have been well meaning, advised you on what to do—without your input and without respect for your own choices? Are you worried that if you even broach the topic of your substance use, you would be advised on how to manage it? It is not uncommon to have such concerns. The reality is that helpers—friends, family, employers, instructors, and others—often try to fix situations with their preferred solution. As a result, you are likely to be cautious about talking about your substance use behaviors, lest you be given advice that you do not want or that does not fit for you.

Motivational interviewing maintains that the person who is considering change is the one who holds the best answer to the problem. After all, it's likely that you have already tried out different approaches and know what works and what has been a dismal failure. Supporting autonomy is about exploring your own ideas for change, as you are an expert on yourself. Keep in mind that you can choose to accept, dismiss, or alter any suggestion provided in this workbook. For example, if I write that "attending a LifeRing group is another secular resource that you have to support your recovery," it is entirely up to *you* whether or not you choose to check out this group. This allows you to make a choice regarding what your next best move might be, because there is no judgment in the statement "It is entirely up to you."

In the exercise that follows, explore the autonomy that you have already experienced as you have made choices to explore your relationship to substances. The ability to determine your own solutions is an important component of feeling empowered and effective. When solutions come from your own source of wisdom, you are more likely to follow through on that solution or find motivation to refine the solution so it becomes effective. That said, we all benefit from having someone to guide us as we explore, especially when that guide knows no one has the answers to our life challenges. Substance use treatment professionals can be sources of important information and processes.

When My Plan Worked

In this exercise, identify a time when you used your own ideas and plans to advocate or complete tasks that were important to you. Here's an example:

Situation: I wanted to visit my ex–boyfriend. We have a difficult relationship, and I am concerned I might start using again.

My own plan	What others recommended	What was the outcome?
To call him and say I would not be able to visit, and I look forward to saying "hi" at a recovery meeting someday.	Cut him off and don't bother with him.	I felt good to choose not to see him and to tell him that I would not be coming over. I did not say anything to my friends who told me to cut him off.

If you could do it over, what would you do differently, if anything? Why?

I would tell my friends that I was going to let him know that I would not be there. I need to stand up for myself in all my relationships.

Possible outcome of your new approach: I would feel more confident and grown up because I can make my own decisions.

Now it's your turn. You can download this worksheet at http://www.newharbinger.com/51901 and complete it as many times as you like.

_____

Situation: _____

My own plan	What others recommended	What was the outcome?

If you could do it over, what would you do differently, if anything? Why?

_____

_____

Possible outcome of your new approach: _____

_____

Now review the example you provided in the worksheet. Looking at the last column, how does your ability to do what needs to be done to reach your goals impact your ability to explore your relationship with substances?

_____

_____

_____

_____

_____

Describe a time when you felt particularly empowered to solve a problem or start a project. How did feeling empowered help you achieve your goal?

_____

_____

_____

_____

_____

In what ways are you empowered to explore your substance use disorder?

_____

_____

_____

_____

Making decisions and moving toward change requires you to have at least some independence. We are all interconnected in this world, but making important decisions about your substance use requires that you believe you have choice and control. Affirming your autonomy helps you recognize that you determine and can change your choices.

Wrap-Up

In chapter 1, acceptance was introduced as a core value of motivational interviewing. In this chapter, we explored the different components of acceptance: absolute worth, affirmation, accurate empathy, and autonomy. Acceptance enables you to explore your relationship to substance use—without judgment, shame, or expectation of specific outcomes. Consider what thinking about acceptance has taught you. What else do you want to learn?

One thing that I learned about myself and acceptance that I can use to explore my relationship to substances is:

_____

_____

_____

_____

One aspect of acceptance that I would like to explore further in order to deepen my understanding of my relationship to substances is:

_____

_____

_____

_____

What's Next?

Now let's move on to address three other important values or attitudes of the spirit of MI: collaboration, empowerment, and compassion. Each will serve you well as you explore your relationship to substance use.

CHAPTER 3

Treat Yourself with Compassion

Acceptance of what is might be a well-known attitude and value associated with change and recovery. But there are more attitudes that invite change. Three more important attitudes help engage us in the change process: *collaboration and partnership, evocation,* and *compassion* (Miller and Rollnick 2023). Like acceptance, each of these ways of thinking allows us to be open to questioning ourselves. Each helps us be more open to and available for change.

To build on your exploration in the previous chapter, notice how and if you accept yourself, and if you are able to show yourself concern and understanding. What comes naturally? What frustrates you? In what ways do you feel at a loss? Are you able to be present for yourself? Describe what your self-acceptance, self-concern, and self-understanding look like when you bring to mind your own substance use:

_____

_____

_____

_____

Compassion for and from Others

Let's begin by looking at how we generally think of compassion. Compassion can be a special time of empathy in which we recognize other people's struggles and take action to help reduce their pain. According to the Tibetan spiritual leader the Dalai Lama, people with the traits of "love, affection, kindness, gentleness, generosity of spirit, and warm-heartedness" are known as *nying je*. They are typically the kind of people who want to practice compassion and help alleviate the suffering of others (Moodian 2016).

Think back to a time in which you felt the pain of others and were moved by this experience. Maybe you felt the pain of someone you read about who suffered a catastrophe half the world away, and you responded by donating resources to a nonprofit organization. Or maybe you deeply felt a coworker's humiliation while he was being yelled at by the boss, so you tried to cheer him up by treating him to lunch. For those of us seeking support with stopping or cutting back on substance use, the connection with another person who is able to show caring and a desire to help us can make a huge difference when physical and social dependency makes it hard to step away from use. When we sense someone's compassion, we are more likely to take a risk and consider how we might do things differently.

Self-Compassion

The concept of self-compassion is becoming more popular as a way to reduce stress and anxiety. Self-compassion, in its most basic form, is a way to give ourselves a break. When we practice self-compassion, we are able to step back and observe our thoughts, feelings, and behaviors that occur in response to all that impacts us. Often when we "watch" ourselves, we are able to get a different point of view. We can see how our decisions and reactions make a lot of sense given the situation in which we made them.

Self-compassion is an important attitude to have when thinking about substance use. We often do things we wish we had not done when we are using, and the shame can result in avoiding the exploration of our substance use. It makes sense that if talking about substance use makes you feel worse, you would rather not talk about substances at all. Given this common experience, it is important to experiment with self-compassion so you can reduce the shame that makes you want to avoid the topic of substance use.

How does compassion show up when working with yourself? Kristin Neff (2023), a leading researcher and author, defines the practice of *self-compassion* as "being supportive to oneself while experiencing suffering or pain." It is one thing to notice and want to alleviate the suffering of others, but willingness to show ourselves compassion can be quite difficult. Depending on personal and cultural issues, we might feel embarrassed, narcissistic, self-pitying, or self-conscious when practicing self-compassion. However, self-compassion increases self-kindness, reminds us of our common humanity, fosters mindfulness, and reduces things like self-judgment, isolation, and overidentification with negative thoughts and judgments (Neff 2023). These all contribute to creating the safety and openness we need to explore substance use. Craig's experience illustrates how self-compassion can help you unhook from judgment and thoughtfully approach your substance use with your perspective and self-respect intact.

★ Craig's Story

One Friday night, Craig calls his friend Jeff in tears. He wants to stop drinking so much on the weekends and throughout the week, and he notices that as he continues to use more alcohol, he feels more desperate and out of control. He is able to tell Jeff that his tears are from the guilt he feels as he keeps thinking over and over about his aggressive and sexual behavior when under the influence. Jeff is very concerned and asks him if he would consider getting help for his drinking, but Craig responds firmly that he does not deserve to be sober. He tells Jeff that he really wants to "take a break" from his partying lifestyle, but he is so ashamed of what he did when under the influence, that he keeps using alcohol to keep punishing himself for all his bad behavior. Jeff encourages Craig to "not be so hard on yourself." Craig is very much focused on punishing himself, and he continues to think constantly about his "bad" behavior.

You may be like Craig, stuck in the cycle of remembering regrettable behaviors and then feeling compelled to punish yourself for these behaviors. It is no surprise that he is tearful, depressed, and anxious. Craig might also run the risk of self-harm and suicide in order to stop the pain of his repetitive thoughts, or *rumination*. Although he likely has a way to go to overcome his compulsive relationship to alcohol, it is essential to step back and forgive himself for what he has done in the past so he can free himself emotionally to move toward the future. Self-compassion will not immediately result in Craig having profound insight about his problematic behaviors, but self-compassion is important because it gives Craig a break from himself.

Many of us are like Craig; we tend to be very hard on ourselves. If being hard on yourself helps you change your behavior, it might be fine. However, it often changes nothing. In fact, being hard on yourself can make the situation worse as your shame and self-loathing can result in a "why should I care" attitude. With such an attitude, change is very difficult because you are not motivated to change, and instead you have a lot of motivation to pretend the issue doesn't exist. In this way, a seemingly little thing like self-compassion can have big results. It can help you realistically, and without shame, face the problem in front of you.

Your Best Thinking Got You Here

A first step in being compassionate toward yourself is to try to understand why you make the decisions you make. Sometimes, it is not always so obvious. Life has a way of being complicated, and many relationship and situational issues can cause us to behave in ways that do not always make sense. However, you can gain self-understanding and compassion by pausing and considering what your behaviors do for you.

For the most part, we try to take good care of ourselves and those we love. Substances can even seem like an initial solution to an issue in our life, even if they became problematic later. Taking a few moments to think about why you started to use substances is often an important first step in building self-compassion and understanding. Let's look at how Craig did this.

Craig is suffering now. He has many regrets about how he changes when he uses alcohol. When he pauses to think about his early days of using alcohol, he sees a different person. The Craig who started to use alcohol when he was sixteen and continued to use alcohol in adulthood was doing so to fit into a peer group and to feel comfortable socializing. Craig had no intention of hurting others or causing major life disruptions. By thinking through who he intended to be—a social and likeable person—versus how he feels about himself now, Craig can step back and get a bit of perspective. When he thinks both about his early intentions around using alcohol and the current outcomes of his alcohol use, he can see himself differently. He is not someone who is intentionally trying to harm others; rather, he is someone who wants to connect with people. Craig now can see that he needs to consider alternative ways to relax when socializing.

This table shows how Craig worked through his history of alcohol use and developed the awareness he now has as the result of this process.

Substance I use: Alcohol

How I feel about my use: I feel guilt and shame

Why did I start to use?	How did it help?	How is it working out now?	How does thinking about my history change how I feel about myself?
I wanted to fit into my peer group and relax.	It did help me connect with people at first. I enjoyed it.	Not good. I don't enjoy it, and I get mean. I've hurt a few people as a result.	I can see how using alcohol was my friend, and I am not a bad person for using it when it helped me get to know people.

Looking at My Relationship with Substances

Now it's your turn. Using your own experience, write in some of your own early intentions around substance use. Notice in the final column how thinking this through has changed your perspective about the situation and yourself. To explore your relationship to multiple substances, you can download this worksheet at http://www.newharbinger.com/51901, and complete it for each substance you are exploring.

Substance I use: _____

How I feel about my use: _____

Why did I start to use?	How did it help?	How is it working out now?	How does thinking about my history change how I feel about myself?

Noticing Self-Compassion

Self-compassion is often developed through some form of perspective taking. Try shifting perspective away from yourself, and your opinions of yourself, toward others. This may allow you to see another perspective of the situation. If you can notice and accept a different perspective, you become open to replacing any negative and destructive views you might be holding toward yourself.

Noticing the Difference Between Perspectives

In this exercise, try to notice the difference between perspectives. Then hold the difference between perspectives with curiosity. You download this exercise at http://www.newharbinger.com/51901.

	Describe a situation in which your substance use was problematic for you.	Write what you said *about* yourself as it relates to this situation.	Write what you might say to a friend if they told you they were in an identical situation.
Example	I woke up not remembering what had happened the night before.	I am a mess. How did I let things get so out of control?	You seem really concerned. I am glad you are okay. Would you like to talk about it?
Situation 1			
Situation 2			
Situation 3			

Read your responses. Notice the difference, if any, between what you said to yourself and what you said to your friend. Write what you noticed—thoughts, feelings, or sensations—here:

_____

_____

_____

Noticing any differences may help you shift to a new place of self-compassion. This opens you up to the contradictions that occur when you are so kind, understanding, and compassionate to others but not to yourself. Over time, you can benefit from returning to this exercise. Consider why you can be open to others but not necessarily to yourself.

Ask yourself, *What do I need to do to be more compassionate toward myself?* Write any thoughts you have about this question here:

_____

_____

_____

The Challenge and Comfort of Self-Compassion

This chapter may have brought you to a place you never visited before. Self-compassion is not often an emotion associated with exploring substance use. You are very likely familiar with many stereotypes and assumptions about people who use substances, and you would not be alone with these ideas. We live in a world where we hold many judgements about substance use, even when many substances are condoned and promoted by the larger culture. It is also possible that you will not feel entirely comfortable with self-compassion when you finish this chapter. This makes sense, as practicing a new behavior or attitude can be awkward. Because of this, have some self-compassion when practicing self-compassion. Giving yourself a break is a big change and will likely take some time to sink in and become more natural.

It takes courage to approach caring for yourself with respect and self-compassion. You might be more accustomed to being hard on yourself, and beating yourself up might feel more comfortable. Such a response is normal, and it is helpful to know that you can return to self-compassion over time in order to become more comfortable with it. Consider Craig's ongoing journey.

Craig had a difficult time accepting that he could show himself some compassion. He found himself resisting being kind to himself or giving himself a break. However, one thing Craig did find helpful was to remember that being self-compassionate did not mean that he should give up his desire to learn more about himself and potentially change his relationship to alcohol. As Craig said to one of his most supportive friends, "I can do both: I have changes to make, and I can give myself credit for trying and not beat myself up as I try things out." Craig found that taking the "both/and" approach to exploring his alcohol use was very helpful. He thought that if he tried to change by cutting back or not using alcohol at various times, he could notice those efforts and give himself credit for trying, even when he feels stuck or disappointed with any setbacks. By being aware of what works out as well as what he needs to change, Craig noticed that he actually felt better about his efforts and more hopeful about his change process.

Consider for a moment your own experience of reading and writing your responses in this chapter. How might you hold a "both/and" approach to exploring your current behavior and while fostering self-compassion?

The following example offers an opportunity to consider how you might build in some self-compassion into your own conversation about changing your substance use. Note: There is no expectation that you will do any or all of the self-exploration activities in the first column.

My Substance Use Exploration Behavior	AND	What I Can Do to Build Self-Compassion
Participate in Dry January (a month of no substance use).	AND	I can recognize any success I had while participating, even if I use some substance during the month.
Go to a 12-step meeting with a friend.	AND	Know that it is okay if I do not connect with all of the ideas at the meeting.
Try to cut back by not using substances one to two days a week.	AND	Know that if I do use the substance during the days I planned to not use, I can still learn a lot from that experience.
Go to a party with the intention of not using any alcohol or drugs.	AND	If for some reason I do use, I can be curious as to why I used alcohol or drugs.

Exploring Substance Use Behavior and Building Self-Compassion

Now it's your turn. The first column has a common topic for self-exploration. The column on the right provides a place for you to write how you might also have self-compassion while doing the hard work of exploring your substance use. The goal of this exercise is to generate some ideas about self-compassion. Add some of your own ideas regarding how you might both consider a new behavior while also being open to the experience of self-compassion. You can download this worksheet at http://www.newharbinger.com/51901.

My Substance Use Exploration Behavior	AND	What I Can Do to Build Self-Compassion
	AND	
	AND	
	AND	
	AND	
	AND	
	AND	

You might have noticed some of the following experiences when completing this exercise:

- You were able to come up with a few different ideas regarding how you might provide self-compassion to yourself.

- You provided self-compassion in terms of offering reassurance if you did not meet an intended goal.

- You stepped back and offered yourself self-compassion in the form of approaching your situation with curiosity or wonder, as in saying to yourself, *I wonder what I meant by that?*

What else did you notice?

_____

_____

_____

_____

_____

_____

_____

The ability to look at ourselves with curiosity instead of judgment and to be flexible in how we approach our behaviors, thoughts, and feelings can also be seen as a type of self-compassion. Think about situations in which you felt especially judged, hurt, or trapped. It is likely that you thought you had few, if any, options to manage your concerns. Imagine if you were able to have some alternative choices, a different point of view, or some way out of your predicament. Pausing for a moment and considering potential options can be an act of compassion as we give ourselves a breather and a moment for considering other ideas or ways to ask for support. Here's what happened for Craig:

Craig noticed that he often feels helpless and enraged by life events and challenges that keep him stuck. He is aware that he has difficulty stopping his drinking once he starts, and he is also embarrassed that he is very much impacted by peer pressure.

Typically, after a night of drinking, Craig spends the next day thinking over and over about what happened the night before and questioning why he cannot stop himself from drinking. If he found himself drinking with someone else, he also stews about how that person was a "bad influence." When Craig goes down this path, he usually experiences a day of angry rumination and shame.

When Craig gave himself an opportunity for reflection and rest, he paused to look at his night. He started to just notice that he gets into drinking situations quite often, and he allowed himself to wonder how he finds himself in such situations. Just to see what he noticed about his situation and behavior, he attempted to step back and look at himself as if he were looking at someone else. Taking this step back allowed him to break some of the relentless self-criticism he engaged in and opened him up to looking at himself and his substance use from an entirely different perspective.

Learning to FAIL

A particularly useful version of this curiosity is approaching any misstep as a "FAIL." The FAIL is different from being a failure, as FAIL stands for "First Attempt in Learning." You can look at a different result than what you wanted or intended as a learning opportunity and *not* as failure. This is a powerful and effective form of self-compassion. To experience the impact of FAIL as a self-compassion tool, let's explore Craig's experience and how the FAIL might work for you.

Craig shared with his friend Jeff how he struggles with feeling that he lets himself and others down all the time. From missed appointments to lack of follow-through on commitments usually resulting from drinking the night before, Craig believes that, more frequently than not, he fails everyone who has supported him. He also worries that he sabotages himself by not being reliable or only doing what he states he will do partway, if at all. During a tearful conversation with Jeff, Craig says he sees himself as a "failure," as he often gets in his own way and keeps himself from making progress with his substance use. He also adds that when he thinks of himself as a failure, he gives up on changing at all. His giving up starts a vicious cycle of more alcohol use, which in turns leads to more failure. He also knows that when he goes down the path of "seeing nothing good about myself," self-compassion is left by the wayside and his self-loathing continues to pile up and contributes to his spiraling into more alcohol use and despair.

Craig found the FAIL exercise to be especially helpful. When he was able to shift his thinking from being a failure to being a learner, he was immediately relieved. Taking on a learner's mindset instead of a loser's identity was a powerful act of self-compassion, and Craig found he was motivated to understand himself better. This self-curiosity also helped him become more interested in changing himself. He found himself looking forward to understanding how he functions and finding ways he could change his relationship with alcohol to make his life better.

Here is how Craig explored this.

How I thought I failed: I drank too much at a party when I wanted to stay sober.

How did I feel?	How was this a first attempt in learning (FAIL)?	How does looking at a FAIL feel different?	What will I do with what I learned from my FAIL?
Embarrassed and angry at myself	I have a hard time not drinking with some of my friends who like to drink and always offer me drinks.	I am not so angry with myself. I can see how I can do something different. I am not helpless.	I will not go to parties with these particular friends when I am trying to avoid drinking. There are at least two people I can talk to and ask them to not drink around me if we spend time together.

How I Learned to FAIL

Now it's your turn. Give your own examples of how your relationship to substances can help you to learn from FAIL (First Attempt in Learning). You can download a copy at http://www.newharbinger .com/51901 so you can fill it out as many times as you like.

How I thought I failed: _____

How did I feel?	How was this a first attempt in learning (FAIL)?	How does looking at a FAIL feel different?	What will I do with what I learned from my FAIL?

Having self-compassion can help you approach conversations about change, as increased compassion comes from and helps promote openness toward yourself and others. Not feeling you deserve to be happy or that you need to pay a price for your substance use can block you from being open to talking about all the opportunities you might have to change your life or think about different ways of living. Shame, or feeling defective in some way, can block attempts to change. Being open to practicing self-compassion helps reduce shame and moves you—and moves us all—toward looking for and engaging other ways to change our lives.

At the beginning of this chapter, you were asked to describe your relationship to accepting yourself, your own self-understanding, and your self-care. Having read this chapter and practiced the exercises, how would you describe your current relationship to yourself?

_____

_____

_____

_____

_____

Recognizing that being open to self-compassion is a process and not an outcome or end point, think of ways you can step forward into your self-discovery while building your own ability to give yourself a break and take some credit for your efforts. Write three ideas:

1. _____

2. _____

3. _____

Finally, exploring your own attitudes toward yourself as well as noticing and possibly accepting the things in life you cannot control can help you let go of attitudes and behaviors that have not helped you when you considered your substance use or life in general. Take a step back to review your experiences completing the exercises and worksheets in this chapter. In what ways are you feeling more clarity and more ability to move forward or create a greater understanding of yourself and your needs?

_____

_____

_____

_____

Having clarity and feeling able are related to self-empowerment. When you are empowered, you are likely more able to behave in ways that allow you to take risks and step forward to do what is needed to help you reach your goals. Having taken these steps, you are on your way to exploring what matters to you and what gives you meaning in life. What gives you meaning is another critical piece of your discovery. You have your own unique combination of values that shape your life, and using your values can help you think through how using substances helps or doesn't help you move toward your values. Examining your substance use in relationship to your values will be the next step in your learning journey.

CHAPTER 4

Let Your Values Fuel Your Journey

You are someone who cares about things. Things like where you live, who you love, and how you spend your time. You have things that you care about in the universe, such as your spiritual beliefs, and things that move you forward in life, such as what kind of education you can complete and what type of work you can perform. For example, some of your "things" could be making sure you spend at least a few hours with friends a week, calling your closest family members at least once a week, practicing yoga daily, and making sure you read for half an hour every night. Consider how you like to spend your time and what you care about. You might know some things you care about that you can write down immediately. Go ahead. Write down at least three things that give you a lot of meaning in your life:

_____

_____

_____

_____

How did that go? Some people find it absolutely overwhelming: How can I write down what is important to me, when it feels as if everything is important to me? Or, you might have thought, *In what situations?* Sometimes you feel it is important to lead and be in charge—for instance, on an important work project. But other times you might prefer to be led and have others do the heavy lifting of providing direction toward a target, like when planning for a holiday dinner. It is also quite possible you might have answered, "I don't really know." We can be very involved in living our lives and doing what we need to do to make ends meet financially, care for children or parents, or just get the day-to-day requirements of living accomplished. If that's the case, you likely do not have a lot of time to think through the larger questions about yourself.

All of these responses, and many more, are completely normal when you are asked to consider what is important to you and what gets you out of bed each and every day. In this chapter, we are going to build some additional awareness around what moves you forward in life. It is likely that you are engaging with this workbook because something needs to shift in your world, and you are questioning your life—as it is. Your relationship with substances threatens things that you care about. Relationships, health, finances, work, or freedom to live without the potential consequences of substance use are often significant concerns.

What you consider meaningful is linked to your values, what you care about in life. The world is full of infinite possibilities regarding how you can live and the choices you can make that ultimately will impact every aspect of your life. When you act based on a set of *values*, or beliefs about how to live life, you are able to set yourself on a life course that is consistent with what you care about.

For example, Joseph values being part of a party "scene." He cares deeply about being the center of attention and showing his friends how to have a good time. He invests time and money into organizing elaborate events and parties, and he pays to have someone document those events in detail for social media. Joseph not only enjoys being in the middle of the party scene and having many people pay attention to him, but he also enjoys streaming his parties and watching the feedback and interaction his party posts receive when he reviews his social media accounts throughout the day.

Jake has different values entirely. Jake is intensely curious, and he loves to learn. He has spent many years in academics, and he teaches philosophy at a community college. Jake reads at least one book a week, and on any given weekend, he can be found reading at home or occasionally in a café. When he has time off from teaching during the summer breaks, his perfect vacation is being at the beach and reading a book a day.

Jake and Joseph have radically different lives, and it is difficult to see any similarities between their lifestyles. What they do have in common is that they both live in a way that is *value driven*. Joseph cares a great deal about being social and spending time with his friends in a party atmosphere, so a vacation at the beach reading books would likely make him miserable. Jake, on the other hand, does everything he can to minimize time at parties or events where he needs to mix with other people. Both lifestyles are perfectly fine. What is important here is that both Jake and Joseph are highly motivated to live their respective lives in these ways because their behaviors are driven by what they value.

Their values provide a conduit for all they do. If aware of their values, they can go through life in ways that help them make choices about what they do based on what they care about. Another way of saying this is that their behavior is highly meaningful for them, and they know what they need to do to engage in what gives their lives meaning and provides them with satisfaction. Their values can be seen as a type of compass that helps move them toward what they desire. They both might have bad days, significant losses such as losing a loved one or important work, and less impactful losses such as unexpected changes in plans or being disappointed. But in the overall path of life, both Jake and Joseph are moving to where they want to go; their values provide a source of motivation and meaning that fuels their life journeys.

Effects of Not Choosing, and Choosing, Your Values

Unlike Jake and Joseph, not everyone is connected to what they value. It can be said, however, that virtually everyone is motivated to move toward *something* in their lives. The motivation does not have to be elaborate or even considered virtuous in the larger culture. Values can be quite simple, and not lofty or difficult to attain, in order to helpful in our lives. So, the issue is not that your values are not "good enough" or complex enough. The problem is not being connected to your values. Being disconnected from values can cause you to make choices you might not have made otherwise, such as doing favors for people who might not have your best interests in mind. Let's say someone asks you to commit fraud. If you are in touch with the values of honesty and integrity, you are more likely to refuse to participate in fraud. Someone who has not really thought about what is important to them might find it confusing or upsetting to set this limit. It can be hard to say "no" to someone, especially if they are close to you or are someone you respect. Without values, you might go along with the request.

It can be a hassle to set a limit and say "no" to any request that might be made, even one that is less impactful than committing fraud. Connecting to your values will make it more likely that the limit will be upheld. Almost everyone can find an example in their lives of a time they acted in a way that they regretted later. Let's look at how this unfolded for Johanna.

★ Johanna's Story

Johanna remembers a time when she said "yes" when instead she should have said "no." Johanna's friend Diane had a cousin who moved to their city earlier that year. Diane was convinced that Johanna and the cousin would hit it off, and she was very excited about the possibility that she might be successful in setting up a couple. Johanna did not think too much about the issue. She did not want to disappoint Diane, and she frankly thought it would be difficult to find a way to decline a date. She told herself, *This isn't that big a deal,* even though she became anxious about meeting the cousin as the date approached. Blind dates are always a risk, and Johanna's experience was not unusual. She met the cousin for drinks at a place her friend arranged, and soon became increasingly uncomfortable. She did not relate to the stories her date told, and she did not like that she was basically excluded from the conversation. Also, he drank a lot, and became increasingly loud and slightly belligerent, which Johanna found offensive. About an hour into the drinks, a terribly long time for Johanna, he asked about going somewhere for dinner. At this point, Johanna found a way out by stating she could only be out for a short time that night as she had an early start in the morning. The date ended somewhat awkwardly. Johanna had an even more awkward time talking with her curious friend Diane the next morning when she had to tell her the whole situation was very distressing for Johanna and not at all what she expected from a date.

Upon reflection, Johanna identified that she had made her choices based on one value: not wanting to disappoint a friend. However, she was also aware that she had other values, which were important to her, that she did not consider, the most important of which was having autonomy in how and when she starts to build relationships. Through this unfortunate experience, Johanna learned a lot about how her values impacted every aspect of her behavior in this situation and how she made choices that went against the values she cares about the most.

Johanna was able to identify her values about initiating relationships. For many people, however, it's not uncommon to care about certain life outcomes—like starting and sustaining a family or nurturing a rewarding career—but not to make any value-based decisions to support such goals. For example, you might have found yourself in situations in which you wondered, *How did I get here?* It might not be surprising how common situations like this are, especially when substances are involved. Consciously or unconsciously, we might *not* be making choices about our lives and behaviors, and by not making choices, we are actually making a choice. We will end up on a path to somewhere, but maybe it is not exactly where we want to be. Here's how it played out for Dale.

★ Dale's Story

Dale got a job out of high school working at a convenience store, and he continued to live at his father's house as it saved him a lot of money as his dad did not charge rent. His living situation worked out fine as he and his dad got along, and he was able to get his basic bills, such as his phone and car insurance, covered with the wages he earned. He got up and went to his job at the convenience store daily. One day he noticed that he was almost thirty years old, he had never changed jobs, and he was still living with his dad. Neither of these situations, occupational or residential, are inherently problematic. What was a problem was that Dale did not actively direct his life based on what he truly valued. He felt stuck, confused, and somewhat hopeless. He was also angry and sad that he had lost time and opportunity to spend time exploring opportunities he might have valued. Finding a partner, taking on a role in the community, or starting a family were all activities Dale thought he might enjoy. But now he was not sure if he had time to fully pursue any of them.

Almost everyone experiences a certain amount of life missteps and inertia. It is impossible, and not even preferable, to plan out every aspect of your life—but how might the decisions of Johanna and Dale have been influenced by their known and cherished values? Johanna can benefit from noticing how she values both friendship and autonomy. This might lead her to communicate better in order to negotiate choices that support her friendships as well as her own interests. If Dale had valued being in close contact with family and having a job where he could be in touch with the community, his current situation might have been entirely satisfying to him. However, if he explored his values and discovered that he values independence and novelty, he might make different choices over time regarding where he worked and lived. Perhaps he would enjoy working in a foreign country, for example.

My Values and How They May Help Me

You might also be thinking about some similar dilemmas in your own life. Use the following worksheet to explore your situation. You can download the worksheet at http://www.newharbinger.com /51901.

Where do you feel stuck?	What is at stake if you do not change?	What might happen if you do change?	What thought, value, or behavior might move you forward?
I don't call my friends when I feel bad. I isolate at home.	I'll become even more lonely and isolated.	I can feel joy about being connected to others.	Love. I love my friends and even some of my coworkers.

Explore the Values That Motivate You

It is not uncommon to find ourselves thinking about our values and life choices when considering our relationship to substances. In fact, using substances can result in consequences—both large and small—that make us wonder if our current behaviors, including substance use, are helping us get to where we want to go. In order to know where you want to go, your challenge might be figuring out what you do value, and when or how you can connect to those specific values. *Values sorting* is a helpful way to clarify the values that motivate you so you can free up this values-driven motivation for change. As a way of considering values, they are often organized by "domains," or areas, such as relationships, career, social or community connections, recreation and leisure, and spirituality, among others (Harris 2021). For example, Johanna chose the life domain of relationship: "In this area of my life, I want to be loving toward others." Dale chose the life domain of work: "In this area of my life, I want to be independent."

Use the following exercise to try values sorting for yourself. It will help you to clarify and explore your values. You can download the exercise at http://www.newharbinger.com/51901.

Sorting My Values

First, think about a situation where you want to apply your values. It might be around a relationship, or you might want to think about what you value in terms of your career. Circle the life domain in which this situation falls:

Career and work

Recreation and leisure

Relationships

Social or community connections

Spirituality

Now complete this sentence:

"In this area of my life, I want to be _____."

Once you have selected an area that you want to focus on, use the values list below to explore how important each value is to you. Next to each value, write whether it is Very Important (VI), Important (I), or Not Important (NI) in relation to your chosen domain. Here are forty common values. There are many more, so please add your own under the "Other" category at the end of the list.

_____ 1. Accepting: open to, allowing of, or at peace with myself, others, life, my feelings, etc.

_____ 2. Adventurous: willing to create or pursue novel, risky, or exciting experiences.

_____ 3. Assertive: calmly, fairly, and respectfully standing up for my rights and asking for what I want.

_____ 4. Authentic: being genuine, real, and true to myself.

_____ 5. Caring/self-caring: actively taking care of myself, others, the environment, etc.

_____ 6. Compassionate/self-compassionate: responding kindly to myself or others in pain.

_____ 7. Cooperative: willing to assist and work with others.

_____ 8. Courageous: being brave or bold; persisting in the face of fear, threat, or risk.

_____ 9. Creative: being imaginative, inventive, or innovative.

_____ 10. Curious: being open-minded and interested; willing to explore and discover.

_____ 11. Encouraging: supporting, inspiring, and rewarding behavior I approve of.

_____ 12. Expressive: conveying my thoughts and feelings through what I say and do.

_____ 13. Focused: focused on and engaged in what I am doing.

_____ 14. Fair/just: acting with fairness and justice—toward myself and others.

_____ 15. Flexible: willing and able to adjust and adapt to changing circumstances.

_____ 16. Friendly: warm, open, caring, and agreeable toward others.

_____ 17. Forgiving: letting go of resentments and grudges toward myself or others.

_____ 18. Grateful: being appreciative for what I have received.

_____ 19. Helpful: giving, helping, contributing, assisting, or sharing.

_____ 20. Honest: being honest, truthful, and sincere—with myself and others.

_____ 21. Independent: choosing for myself how I live and what I do.

_____ 22. Industrious: being diligent, hardworking, dedicated.

_____ 23. Kind: being considerate, helpful, or caring—to myself or others.

_____ 24. Loving: showing love, affection, or great care—to myself or others.

_____ 25. Mindful/present: fully present and engaging in whatever I'm doing.

_____ 26. Open: revealing myself, letting people know my thoughts and feelings.

_____ 27. Orderly: being neat and organized.

_____ 28. Persistent/committed: willing to continue, despite problems or difficulties.

_____ 29. Playful: being humorous, fun-loving, light-hearted.

_____ 30. Protective: looking after the safety and security of myself or others.

_____ 31. Respectful/self-respectful: treating myself or others with care and consideration.

_____ 32. Responsible: being trustworthy, reliable, and accountable for my actions.

_____ 33. Skillful: doing things well, utilizing my knowledge, experience, and training.

_____ 34. Supportive: being helpful, encouraging, and available—to myself or others.

_____ 35. Trustworthy: being loyal, honest, faithful, sincere, responsible, and reliable.

_____ 36. Trusting: willing to believe in the honesty, sincerity, reliability, or competence of another.

_____ 37. Other: _____

_____ 38. Other: _____

_____ 39. Other: _____

_____ 40. Other: _____

Once you are done writing in your codes (VI, I, NI), look at all those that you consider VI, or very important. Are there three to five very important values that are especially meaningful to you regarding the situation you thought of earlier? For example, Johanna chose to sort out her values regarding relationships. For her, the top values included "trust," "autonomy," "communication," "respect," and "honesty." Knowing these values, Johanna was able to see how any blind date required her to give up some autonomy and trust when she did not feel comfortable in doing so. For Johanna, in her story above, not communicating with her date was also not consistent with her values, and she found his drinking significant amounts of alcohol offensive and disrespectful. All of this was enough information for Johanna to know that this entire situation was not a good fit for her. She was now clear that in the future she would be best served by declining to go on blind dates and finding other ways to connect with potential romantic partners.

Write your top three to five values here:

1. _____

2. _____

3. _____

4. _____

5. _____

Were you surprised by the values you chose? Why or why not?

_____

_____

Sometimes we are surprised by our values simply because we have been living without much awareness of them. On the other hand, we might not be surprised by our values because they are always functioning in the background of what we do—we just need to be made aware of them.

Working with Your Chosen Values

Now that you have a sense of your values, select three to five of your most important values, and consider thinking through the following issues. Use the example in the first line as a guide.

My value and life domain	How does living by this value help me be who I want to be?	Example of how this value helps me make choices that help me be who I want to be	How might my value help me avoid choices that I might regret?
Example: Loving: being a better parent	I won't be as mean to my kids.	I will think through the different ways to discipline my kids.	I will think about how what I say might hurt someone's feelings.

In almost any situation, working with values can help provide much needed clarity when you find yourself stuck and not sure what to do next. For the next exercise, we will consider values in relationship to substance use.

How Values Relate to My Substance Use

For this values sorting exercise, you will choose your values based on your relationship to substances.

This time, sort the values using this prompt:

"In regard to substance use, I want to be _____ "
(Harris 2021).

Using the previously offered list of forty values, notice what comes up in this sorting. Are there any differences or similarities in your values that you chose for the other areas of your life? You might notice that you have some core values that show up in most areas of your life, and those values will be especially important in helping you move forward regarding your decisions around using substances. You might also notice some differences in values, and you might wonder why you have different values when considering substance use. Completing this values table can help you sort out how substance use helps, or does not help, you live in line with your values.

My value in relationship to substance use	How does living by this value impact my substance use?	How does this value help me make choices that help me be who I want to be?	How might my value help me avoid choices that I might regret?
Example: Integrity	I don't want to be using coke so much that I lose control and start ripping off friends.	I might be inclined to not use it in some intense party situations where I might lose control if I use too much.	I can remind myself to be up-front and honest when considering if it is a good idea for me to use on any given night.

As you continue to explore your relationship to substances in this workbook, remember that values are a key piece to any decision you make. Values are powerful, as they tend to remain steady, even when we apply different values to various life situations.

In our lives, we will experience a multitude of emotions based on the ups and downs of being human: relationships ending and beginning, illness and pain, loss, various levels of stress and trauma, wonder, excitement, and joy, just to name a few. Our experiences and feelings come and go, but our values are with us regardless of what life brings us. We might not always be delighted with our life circumstances, but we can always connect with our values and rely on them to lead us toward the light and the next steps on our journey. Knowing what you value might also fuel your interest in further exploring your relationship to substances. The next step in this exploration will allow you to reflect on what is most important to you on your journey of self-understanding. Knowing what you think and feel can help you decide how to relate to substances and assist you in determining your next steps toward change.

CHAPTER 5

Listen to Yourself

You have formed the basis of an effective exploration of change: an open, nonjudgmental, collaborative attitude. You have already explored your own attitude and values, and possibly you are starting to have more clarity about how your substance use has both benefits and costs in your life. In this chapter, you will move from exploring what you care about to having a conversation with yourself. With a set of simple skills, you can move from your current status (such as current substance use), through any "stuckness" you might feel about changing (like feeling two ways about something), to making a step toward change. These microskills you will learn in this book are taught and used by many helping professionals, with more than seventy years of research supporting their effectiveness (Miller and Moyers 2021). They directly or indirectly support the values and attitudes that promote our conversation about change in this workbook. Jonas's story gives us an example of how such skills might be used.

> Jonas is aware that he cares about being a good friend and parent. He has noticed many judgments about times his partner kicked him out of their house for coming home under the influence of alcohol and other drugs. He also knows he has enjoyed partying in the past, and he can honestly state that he loves his friends who use drugs. Jonas is stuck. He has self-compassion for himself, and he knows he needs to change something in his life, but he needs to explore these issues further. He's curious about his feelings and what changing means to him. He wants to be OK with the fact that he really loves to party, and he also wants to keep a relationship with his partner and children. Reflecting on his relationship is a skill that Jonas can use to listen to himself. The more he explores, the more opportunity he has to develop clarity on his next steps.

Let's start with the skill of reflection. You can observe your own emotions and possibly what your emotions mean as if you are supporting another person. Learning how to reflect on your own process is a skill that enables you to come into contact with deeper and more profound levels of meaning and understanding. It's an open process of being curious and wondering, *What do I mean by this?*

When a helping professional uses reflection with a client, this is occasionally called "mirroring." After a client speaks, the therapist may offer a paraphrase of what they heard, which enables the client to feel understood. Because they feel seen or understood, the client is more inclined to delve deeper into their story. With deeper dives comes the possibility of greater understanding and awareness of a dilemma, and the person potentially arrives at insight and motivation to change. For instance, if you are speaking with a helper about how you and your boss had an argument about your coming in late, the helper might offer a reflective response such as, "You are frustrated that you and your boss did not see eye to eye this morning, and having a tense conversation has left you worried about the status of your job". In such a conversation, you might not have specifically mentioned the frustration or worry, but the listener was able to see nonverbal expressions and behaviors, and hear your actual words, to mirror back the meaning and feeling of what you said.

Most of the time, we respond to such empathy by automatically continuing to speak and move further into our dilemma. It is not something you might be conscious of doing, but accurate empathy allows you to feel safe because you are being understood. Greater psychological understanding typically leads to more conversation. The more you explore, the more you learn about yourself and pathways to change have a greater chance of emerging.

Over time, the pioneering humanistic psychologist and researcher Carl Rogers came to believe that a reflective statement needs to be tentative and considerate of the possibility that the listener is not entirely correct. It needs to come from a place of humility, not overconfidence. An empathic attitude like this can shape the reflective response, even when engaging yourself in your own reflections. A humble and empathically connected listener is more curious and thoughtful about their reflective statement, and all reflective statements are grown out of a sincere attempt to connect (Arnold 2014). The reflective listening response communicates "I am trying to understand you," not "I am telling you that this is the way you think and feel." By coming to any conversation, with yourself or others, with curiosity and a genuine desire to understand, insight and meaning can emerge in the exchange between listener and speaker. Such an exchange offers psychological safety and opens up a conversation that can grow through collaboration and respect. While it's helpful to engage in this type of conversation with a trusted person, the most important ongoing conversation you have is with yourself. Using reflective listening, you can learn to empathically listen and respond to yourself.

You can use a number of reflective listening skills to promote a complex conversational exchange with yourself. By "complex," we mean that it goes more deeply into what you are thinking and feeling, which helps you understand yourself and your actions more fully. With greater understanding and the use of these reflection skills, you will eventually be able to answer the questions: *What do I need to do to address my relationship with substances? How do I get there? What might I be willing to do next?*

The reflective listening interventions in this workbook can provide you with a process to explore your own answers in a way that is meaningful and productive for you. In this chapter, we will draw on four types of reflective listening skills from motivational interviewing to help you create meaningful complex reflection: peeling the onion, continuing the paragraph, metaphor, and double-sided reflection. These skills can help your reflective process regarding your relationship with substances (Miller and Rollnick 2023). Let's get started.

Peeling the Onion

Like an onion, each of us is multilayered and so are our conversations (Rosengren 2017). Consider this question: "What might you be willing to explore in order to learn more about your relationship with alcohol?" This open-ended question offers endless possibilities for responding. Let's say someone says, "I would like to look more at my history of drinking. I started when I was twelve, and I loved it. I always felt like I was part of something every time I drank. I never felt alone. I liked that, and I still do."

This statement is at the surface of the onion, the red or yellow cellophane-like skin covering the vegetable. To reflect on this statement, we want to first think about what kind of statements this person would potentially make if we were able to peel back some of the onion layers. For instance, in this example, it is quite possible that underneath the top layer, we might find some of the following statements:

- I want to understand why I need to use alcohol in order to not feel alone.

- I like using alcohol because it helps me be a part of something and being a part of something is still really important to me.

- I need to understand how alcohol is able to help me feel less isolated.

Each of these statements reflects on a slightly different component of the statement. Which one of these statements is correct? All of these statements can be correct!

Listeners might come up with these statements as hypotheses regarding what the speaker means. They would then shift the "I" to a "you" and reflect back to the speaker one of these statements: "It seems possible that you like using alcohol because it helps you be a part of something, and being a part of a community, group, or activity is really important to you." It is important to note that the listener generates such a response after spending some time connecting with the listener. The listener becomes empathically engaged in such a way that they are humble in the delivery of the reflection. The listener is able to reconstruct the reflection if the speaker indicates that they are off, and in this way the empathic and active reflection process is cocreated by listener and speaker.

Speaker: Well, yes, it is important that I can connect to people now, but I just wonder how it all began for me. What was going on for me at age twelve that made drinking so compelling?

Listener: Yes, you are trying to understand your history and how alcohol was able to be so seductive when you were so young.

Speaker: Yes. That's what I want to know.

Exercise: Peeling the Onion

The goal of this exercise is to think about what we can "hear" in various statements and identify possible self-reflection statements. Simply try to come up with some possible statements given what you think might be a deeper meaning for the speaker. In a "real life" situation, you would have more immediate context that would help you shape your responses.

After each statement, write two to four sentences that could possibly reflect a deeper meaning for the statement.

1. I don't know why everyone is on my case about my partying on the weekends (and Thursday nights). Everyone I work with is drinking just as much as me, and I have a job where I need to keep up with my team…in every way possible.

    _____

    _____

    _____

    _____

2. I have cut back on how often I go to the dispensary. Earlier this year, I would be going to the dispensary almost every day. I think everyone can agree that I have been making some important steps in cutting back.

    _____

    _____

    _____

    _____

3. I have been using Percocet for pain since the accident. I don't appreciate my doctor telling me I have to cut back. I need them for pain. I am not abusing my pain meds.

    _____

    _____

    _____

    _____

4. I am not drinking too much. Everyone at my school drinks at least a six-pack of beer per person a night. It is just how much people drink when they go to college. I am tired of being hassled about it.

    _____

    _____

    _____

    _____

Review your responses. How hard was it for you to come up with at least a couple of responses? The more we practice creating responses, the more skilled we become at recognizing and speaking to some of the underlying meaning.

Exercise: Peeling Your Own Onion

Now that you have a bit of practice, we'll shift to helping you work with peeling down some of your own statements. Use the prompts here to explore your own statements about your relationship with substances.

Prompt 1: Why did you choose to work through this workbook?

_____

_____

_____

Peel that onion. What else does your answer mean?

_____

_____

_____

Prompt 2: What types of behaviors, feelings, or thoughts have you had about exploring your relationship to substances?

_____

_____

_____

Peel that onion. What else does your answer mean?

_____

_____

_____

Prompt 3: What have you already done to change your relationship to substances?

_____

_____

_____

Peel that onion. What else does your answer mean?

_____

_____

_____

Prompt 4: What would you have to gain or lose by changing your relationship to substances?

_____

_____

_____

Peel that onion. What else does your answer mean?

_____

_____

_____

As you worked on this exercise, you might have noticed the interaction of the open-ended questions and the reflections that follow them. The questions engage us in exploration, and the reflections help us make sense of the exploration and then encourage us to go deeper. This curious and in-depth approach will typically generate change talk, and it is this change talk that will move you down your chosen and valued pathway to change. Now that we've "peeled the onion," let's explore some other reflective listening formats. These will offer ways for you to approach thoughts, feelings, and the meaning concerning various dilemmas, which can help deepen your thoughts about change.

Continuing the Paragraph

The continuing the paragraph reflection anticipates what a person might say if they were to continue their reflection. Many of these types of responses begin with "and," "so," or "yet," as the listener adds to what was just shared. Here are two examples to illustrate how a continuing the paragraph reflection might work.

Example 1:

> *Speaker:*   I am not sure how I feel about quitting smoking. I don't want to experience withdrawals, but I also am so over it.

> *Listener:*   …and you would like to find a way to approach withdrawals so you can deal with smoking once and for all and not be controlled by it anymore.

Example 2:

> *Speaker:*   I have been smoking cannabis for so long that it is hard for me to imagine what it might be like to not smoke it.

> *Listener:*   …so, you are really unsure what your life might be like without cannabis.

Such reflections might continue to engage the speaker in further exploration. You also may see how such a reflection can be oriented toward change talk. In the first example, the listener reflects back, and the phrase "so you can deal with smoking once and for all and not be controlled by it anymore" is a reason for change. MI practitioners are thoughtful about not reflecting too much change talk too soon, as doing so can move someone *away* from change. The process of moving away from change, even when we really need to make change, is a part of the ambivalence. Consider times when you have been given really good advice, but you just cannot take it. Many times, that occurs because it is given too soon in your change process. We often need time to consider aspects of our current situation (or the "status quo") before we can start to embrace aspects of change.

In the second example, it might be anticipated that the speaker would need to spend some time exploring their status quo. While doing such exploration, maybe the reasons, needs, desires, abilities, and steps toward change talk will start to emerge. Since you are doing your own reflection in this process, be prepared to pick out some of the change talk in your reflections in this exercise:

Exercise: Practice Continuing the Paragraph

The sentences below are possible statements made by someone talking about their relationship to substances. Your job is to come up with a "continuing the paragraph" reflection. Consider what you might say next that would add to and extend what the person just said.

1. *I don't think I have a problem with drinking, but my partner says she is worried about me.*

   What might you continue with? Consider starting with "and," "so," or "yet."

   _____

2. *I sometimes borrow my kid's Ritalin. I don't do it that often, and he doesn't miss it as he never runs out.*

   _____

3. *I have been wondering about just stopping all drugs and alcohol for a while. I know that other people do it, and it is even kind of popular right now.*

   _____

4. *I want to be a good role model for my kids. As they get older, I anticipate they will ask about alcohol and drugs. They might even ask me if I have used alcohol and drugs. I don't want to get caught off guard.*

   _____

5. *I am ready to stop drinking, I really am. I still like to micro-dose with acid (LSD) now and again. I think going on a trip is good for me.*

   _____

What did you write down? Here are some other possible responses.

1. And her concerns have you possibly thinking about your own relationship with alcohol.

2. So, you are feeling confident you are not overusing Ritalin, and you are paying attention to how your use might impact your child.

3. And you are wondering if maybe taking a break from alcohol and drugs is the right move for you right now.

4. So, you are starting to think through how your behavior impacts your kids and how they might even confront you some on your use.

5. So, you are feeling comfortable with your LSD use, and you are noticing you are potentially getting prepared to make a big change with alcohol by giving it up.

As you look at these possible responses and compare them to your own, please note that there are many possible ways to respond to such statements. No single answer is the absolute correct answer. When you write such reflective statements, do know that you will have context that will help shape your response. Also notice any judgments that might emerge for you. For instance, it is likely that you had a strong response to my reflection of statement #2 (regarding Ritalin use). For many of us, there are a number of personal boundary violations, and even legal and ethical issues here. In a clinical setting, these would eventually be addressed. The task of reflection is how to provide some meaning to what the person says in order for them to feel heard. Once engaged, we can then explore the impact of behaviors, their values, and possible options.

Metaphors

Metaphor reflections are those in which a figure of speech or illustration is symbolic of the issue at hand, but the statement is not an actual representation of the situation. A common metaphor almost everyone in the United States might recognize is "caught between a rock and a hard place." When we first heard this metaphor, we may have had an image of someone or something being literally stuck between a large rock or boulder and a wall. Now we know that the statement means someone is in a difficult situation in which escape is not easy, if it's possible at all.

The metaphor reflection is useful as it helps us recognize our own dilemma through the metaphor. For many of us, hearing an accurate metaphor to describe our situation can be powerful as it shows understanding of the situation while not directly talking about it. A metaphor, by illustrating or otherwise speaking to or pointing out a connection between the statement and your situation, creates a moment of recognition and potentially a deeper understanding. You may experience a sense of relief or even joy when what you are experiencing is reflected in metaphor. It can be an "aha" moment that leads to more interest in exploring further. Coming up with a metaphor for your situation will also help you understand the nature of your dilemma, which in turn deepens your understanding of your needs and motivations.

Consider these common metaphors. What types of situations do you think they refer to?

1.   *I am tired of being on an emotional roller coaster.*

2.   *Joseph told me the story of how he hit bottom.*

3.   *I have had it. I am at the end of my rope.*

4.   *I notice that I am attracted to alcohol as it gives me liquid courage.*

Although one's culture or familiarity with these metaphors might influence one's understanding of them, many of us would interpret these statements like this:

1.   Having emotional ups and downs (like the roller coaster).

2.   "Hitting bottom" is a term made famous by the 12-step program. It is the recognition that one has had so many significant consequences from their substance use that they cannot go further down, and they are compelled to seek help after losing as much as they have. (Different people have different "bottoms.")

3.   Being at the end of one's rope refers to being at a place where someone is entirely fed up and not willing to tolerate the status quo.

4.   Liquid courage refers to the power of alcohol to disinhibit. One might not be open to talking to others, for instance, but drinking alcohol loosens them up enough so they feel "courage" to talk.

Metaphors can be long or only a couple of words. Many metaphors are so ingrained in our language and conversation that we might not even identify them as metaphors until we stop to consider them.

Jonas was able to create a couple metaphors for his own challenge. In order to come up with the metaphor, Jonas spent a few moments with his eyes closed, thinking about how his relationships to substances felt. He spent a few moments noticing any images that came up. Here are Jonas's metaphors: "I'm in a tug of war between my friends and my family and I keep finding myself pulled between the two sides" and "I feel torn, like a sheet down the middle, between my friends and my family members."

Exercise: Finding a Metaphor for Your Substance Use

Consider your own relationship with substances. What is a metaphor that illustrates your relationship to the substance or a current challenge you are having with the substance? The metaphor might be a common metaphor used in everyday language, or it can be something you create.

_____

_____

As you read your metaphor, write what you have learned about your relationship with substances.

_____

_____

_____

Is there anything that surprised you about what you learned from your metaphor? Any next steps you might want to take?

_____

_____

_____

_____

_____

The Double-Sided Reflection

The double-sided reflection is a very useful tool for mirroring the challenges associated with being ambivalent. The double-sided reflection has this name because it is constructed to reflect on the status quo, while also inserting a reflection on change. If you are ambivalent, you are stuck between the status quo and wanting to change your current situation. The double-sided reflection acknowledges the fact that there are compelling reasons for the status quo to exist while you are also starting to become interested in change.

The double-sided reflection gradually promotes change talk intentionally while also acknowledging that the current state of things also exists. This can be thought of as a way to recognize the "both/and" of our lives: *I can love using cannabis,* and *I can also be so over it.* Say I only acknowledge the things that I am okay with now, for instance, a history of enjoying cannabis use. Then I will stay immersed in the current state of things, even if I know that I would also like to experience another reality or break from the things I do not like. On the other hand, if I go too far and fast toward focusing on change, I can feel too "pushed" and resist changing. If I can hold both, then I am in a better position to be open to new possibilities while I am honest about attachment to my current behavior.

Acknowledging this reality is important because when you are able to acknowledge that two things seemingly so different can actually be true at the same time, you can relax and not have to be so concerned with defending the "good" and "not so good" aspects of your substance use. When you are able to be okay with both the beneficial and potentially problematic qualities being true at the same time, it allows you to be open to many more options for changing your relationship to substance use. For instance, it can be true that Jonas likes to party with friends every weekend. Jonas also knows that when he drinks every weekend, he usually loses one full day to recovering. Once Jonas accepts both are true, he does not have to spend time trying to defend (to himself or others) that he likes to use drugs and drink with his friends. Once he can "hold" that fact without shame, he can be open to thinking about how he can explore his relationship to drugs and alcohol given this reality. The next exercise can help you understand this "both/and" process in your own life.

Exercise: My Double-Sided Reflection

Think about an aspect of your substance use that you feel ambivalent about changing. If nothing immediately comes to mind, try this exercise anyway and see what emerges for you as you ask yourself these questions. Complete the left- and right-hand columns in this table.

A substance you are using: _____

My Substance Use Exploration Behavior	AND	What I Can Do to Build Self-Compassion
Example: I like the way I can sleep at night when I smoke weed.	AND	I smoke too much, and I am not motivated to do much in the morning.
	AND	
	AND	
	AND	
	AND	
	AND	

How does looking at both the current status of your relationship to the substance and reasons to change impact your willingness to continue to explore change?

_____

_____

What do you feel about this process?

_____

_____

What are your current thoughts about your substance use?

_____

_____

What would you like to do next?

_____

_____

You have now worked through some of the first and maybe most important skills of motivational interviewing—being able to reflect back meaning and feeling to yourself. Notice how it feels to step back and reflect on parts of yourself that are curious and open to exploring. Think about how it might move you forward in understanding what you want to do next for yourself.

Consider returning to these reflective exercises as you notice new insights or feelings about your substance use. The reflections are helpful for self-understanding and getting unstuck from choices you might change or not change. Insight is part of moving forward in your exploration. You might want to make a change, and you might also find yourself not feeling confident in your ability to make a move. In the next chapter, you will explore your strengths, and you will have an opportunity to think through how your strengths can help empower you to take small or big steps toward being the person you hope to be.

CHAPTER 6

Notice Your Strengths

Your strengths have gotten you through so much. We all have strengths, no matter how much we or others might doubt them. It's not only important for you to acknowledge your strengths, but also essential to know which strengths you rely on in your life. In this chapter, we'll explore the role your strengths play in how you approach change.

First, it's important to share why acknowledging your strengths is different from affirming yourself through encouraging statements. You may think that an affirmation is a simple or even sappy "feel good" statement that misses the mark—like "You can do anything you set your mind to." Affirmation in motivational interviewing, however, has a different focus. MI supports affirmation by noticing and reflecting back your strengths, abilities, skills, achievements, awards, accomplishments, talents, and anything else that demonstrates your individual value and ability. The affirmation practice in MI differs from a standard boosting via praise, promise, and hope. Instead, it focuses on characteristics, skills, and abilities that can be seen and acknowledged, typically in behavior. In fact, the behavior, and the possible outcome of that behavior, can be very meaningful to you so you are more likely to believe the sincerity of this kind of affirmation.

Consider the affirmation "I will prosper" that an online affirmation generator created. We might use the affirmation to notice one of your qualities. Instead of "I will prosper," you can shift that statement to "I am someone who is very aware of my resources—my talents, my support systems, and my skills—and I think carefully about how I use them." This second statement is not a guarantee that you will prosper (outcome), but it acknowledges something you do (good resource management) that would likely put you on the path of achieving a prosperous future.

In MI, an affirming statement is something personally meaningful that supports your confidence with decisions and abilities. We might shift the affirmation "I believe in myself" into "I have been able to get myself out of tough situations in the past, and I have confidence that I will be able to problem-solve what I need to do in order to help myself in the future." Can you feel the difference between the two statements? The first statement could easily be challenged: What makes you think you can believe in yourself? The second statement offers proof to as to why you would make such a statement: *I have confidence because I have a history of prior success.* This shows how we can add specificity to make our statements more believable and personally meaningful. For example, instead of saying, "I am capable," I can be more specific about what it is that makes me aware of my capabilities. Here are some examples:

- I am able to solve my own problems when stuck.

- I am often sought out to help others address their concerns.

- I have achieved _____ in my life.

- I have survived very difficult times.

- I have raised three strong adults.

In fact, there are infinite examples of how we can demonstrate our capability.

Not everyone is comfortable with affirmation—not only because it can feel fake, but also because it can be overwhelming. For instance, we might be caught off guard by a perceived compliment or praise. Even if the statement is a description, it is not uncommon to feel self-conscious or unworthy of positive affirmation. For instance, Tad found himself very self-conscious when his professor pointed out that he had the highest score on a math exam. Although he worked hard on the test, he was uncomfortable being singled out for attention when he knew his peers also studies very hard preparing for the exam. What causes such discomfort? We can feel that we are undeservedly taking credit. Consider your own culture and messages about self-acknowledgment that you might have received growing up. It is not uncommon to be from a culture that discouraged you from taking credit for your own accomplishments. Instead, you may feel embarrassed, guilty, or ashamed when you receive individual attention that acknowledges your gifts. Let's look at how Tegan felt when they were introduced to affirmation.

★ Tegan's Story

The idea of finding affirmations or strengths brings up both fear and annoyance as Tegan "doesn't really see the point." Tegan has a history of methamphetamine use, which they recovered from in their early twenties. Now forty-three, Tegan is questioning their cannabis use. Tegan usually uses cannabis at the end of the day to relax. On the weekends, they can use more cannabis as they have more free time without the pressures of work or of getting their children to and from school. Tegan is quite guarded about their cannabis use as they feel guilty about "having another problem." They are concerned that family members might show concern or bring up substance use as more evidence that Tegan is not able to care for themselves and their family. Tegan has been in therapy for many years since leaving the substance use treatment program about twenty years ago. Although they appreciate the supportive relationship with their therapist, Tegan feels challenged to name anything they have contributed to their growth in the last couple of decades. Tegan knows they have made great strides, but they are much more comfortable giving credit to their partner and family for their success. When asked why they might feel this way, Tegan spoke of feeling so much pain for being such a burden to the family and bringing shame on the family when they were unhoused for about a year at the height of their addiction. Overall, Tegan believes they are a "failure," and they are lucky to have been in a family that has been so active and supportive in their care.

Affirmation helps us locate our strengths and achievements. It builds on our belief that we have what it takes to achieve a goal, and it is characterized by our sense of confidence. If I don't believe I have what it takes to achieve a particular goal, I feel low confidence and little sense of being able to complete a task or achieve a goal. Alternatively, when I am confident, and I identify as being able to achieve my goal, it will increase my likelihood of moving toward identifying and achieving goals.

Let's consider the role and impact of affirmation and confidence in your life. Think for a moment about what might help build and sustain confidence for you.

How confident do you generally feel toward completing tasks or goals in your life?

_____

_____

What do you think impacts your confidence?

_____

_____

_____

_____

What kinds of things help promote your confidence?

_____

_____

_____

In what ways are you able or not able to accept it when people affirm your skills, abilities, and achievements?

_____

_____

Your Strengths Milestones

You have grown and changed so much in your life. For now, believe me when I say that your history is full of reasons to feel confident. Think about your accomplishments, awards, and achievements. Important life accomplishments required you to apply your strengths to complete a significant task. These are your milestones. Milestones help you see the big picture of how you applied your strengths to make progress in your life. Describe your milestones for what they are, instead of judging them. For instance, if I think, *I only completed high school*, my phrasing might cause me to think that completing high school is not worthy of including on a list of strengths when it is, in fact, a huge milestone! If you judge a milestone negatively, you won't include it when you explore your strengths. So approach this exercise by first acknowledging the things you have accomplished.

Let's explore how you can use milestones to build confidence in your ability to grow and change. When asked, Tegan came up with this list of life events that they connected to as achievements.

1. As a young child, I learned English after learning Portuguese from my mom.

2. I finished elementary school, even though I struggled with a limited curriculum and teachers who did not understand my neurodivergence.

3. I understood I was trans when I was sixteen and took care of myself until I was able to come out at age twenty-eight.

4. I finished high school.

5. I survived being unhoused.

6. I met my spouse, and we have had a loving relationship for almost a decade.

My Milestones List

How about you? Here is your opportunity to create a detailed list for yourself of all the ways you have survived and thrived to become the person you are now. You might be able to remember some smaller accomplishments and you will likely remember the milestones that marked a certain time of your life, such as having your own child. Both are important, and try to remember all you can to build your unique list. Start at the beginning of your life and list your amazing human development! If you need extra space, write in your journal or on a large sheet of paper.

Making a detailed list can be powerful, and it can help motivate you. Also, things that seem "negative"—remember to avoid judgment!—can usually be reframed as strength or resilience. We are not assessing here whether or not a life event should or should not have happened. We are giving you credit for your human experience of surviving, developing resilience and grit, and letting your strengths support you.

1. _____

2. _____

3. _____

4. _____

5. _____

6. _____

7. _____

8. _____

9. _____

10. _____

Did you come up with ten milestones that you can celebrate? If not, keep thinking! Once you are done, read through your list. Without self-editing, what comes up for you regarding who you are and what your skills and abilities are? If you had describe yourself in a few words on a name badge, what would you write?

Hello, I am _____ and _____ and _____.

Now go through your list and start to pick out the various strengths that your milestones indicate. Tegan chose the following strengths:

- intelligence (demonstrated by learning a second language)

- attentiveness (a skill honed by learning a second language)

- resilience (gained by finishing high school without the support they needed from teachers)

- strength (shown by finishing high school without additional learning support)

- honesty (committed to when being honest to self about identity)

- courage (demonstrated by coming out to others and staying true to their identity)

- resourcefulness (shown by being able to live on the streets)

- humility (honed by being able to learn about recovery for methamphetamine use)

- loving (demonstrated in their relationship with their spouse)

This is just a partial list. Do you notice any other strengths that Tegan has that are not already on this list? Add them here:

_____

_____

_____

You might have already noticed that an important part of doing this exercise is explicitly *identifying* these strengths because the strengths are there, even though you may not notice them. While you can also notice any judgments about yourself for noticing strengths (for example, "It was not that big a deal to graduate from high school"), the judgment does not make the milestone any less real. Write your strengths inventory from your own milestones list here.

1. _____

2. _____

3. _____

4. _____

5. _____

6. _____

7. _____

8. _____

9. _____

10. _____

You might notice that the milestones list is longer than you expected, and that your strengths list is long as well. The long lists are an indication that you have survived as an accomplished human. You want to be able to take in all of those accomplishments. The long strengths list describes much about who you are, so sit with that feeling. Try to notice any judgments that come up, and if they do come up, try not to judge the judging (Linehan 1993). Practice saying to yourself, *I am aware that I have a judgment about this right now, and that that is okay. I am just listing my history.*

Let's look at another source of inspiration as you identify your strengths. On the next page is a list of common strengths (Spacey 2021). Which ones have you noticed in yourself? Circle all that apply.

Ability to execute

Accountability

Accuracy

Action oriented

Adaptable

Agent of change

Ambition

Analysis

Art

Athletic ability

Attention span

Attention to detail

Big-picture thinking

Bravery

Budget control

Budget planning

Build rapport

Build relationships

Business acumen

Business knowledge

Business planning

Calculated risk
  taking

Challenging
  assumptions

Challenging the
  status quo

Change
  management

Civility

Coding

Collaboration

Commitment

Communication

Compassion

Competence

Competitive

Confidence

Conflict
  management

Consensus building

Constructive
  criticism

Continuous
  improvement

Cooperation

Coordination

Creativity

Credibility

Critical thinking

Cross-cultural
  communication

Curiosity

Dealing with
  ambiguity

Dealing with
  difficult people

Debate

Decision making

Delivering
  commitments

Dependable

Design sense

Design thinking

Determination

Difficult
  conversations

Digital literacy

Diligence

Emotional
  intelligence

Empathy

Energy

Engagement

Enthusiasm

Entrepreneurship

Experience

Facilitation

Fast learner

Financial
  management

Flexibility

Forecasting

Friendliness

Goal planning

Grit

Handling criticism

Handling stress

Helpful

Humor

Imagination

Independent

Industrious

Influential

Integrity

Interest

Introspection

Intuition

Inventive

Leadership

Learning from
  mistakes

Listening

Loyal

Magnetic
  personality

Mentorship

Objective view of
  self

Objectivity

On time

Open

Optimistic

Organized

Originality

Passionate

Patience

Persistent

Personal presence

Personal resilience

Persuasion

Physical strength

Play

Politeness

Positive attitude

Pragmatic

Problem-solving

Productivity

Professionalism

Rational

Realistic

Reliable

Resourceful

Respectful

Responsible

Self-control

Self-directed

Self-improvement

Social skills

Stable

Stylish

Taking initiative

Team building

Technical
  proficiency

Thinking ahead

Tolerance for
  differences

Tough

Troubleshooting

Trustworthy

Unbiased

Understanding

Willingness to learn

Read the strengths you have circled. Notice what emotions or thoughts you have as the result of reading this list and allowing yourself to connect to your strengths based on your history.

What are you feeling now?

_____

_____

_____

What are you thinking about yourself?

_____

_____

_____

_____

What sensations do you experience in your body?

_____

_____

How might these feelings, thoughts, and sensations contribute to exploring your relationship to substances?

_____

_____

_____

_____

_____

If you are noticing negative judgments when reviewing your strengths, pause here and bring aware-ness to the judgment. If you are able, become curious about the judgment and take a moment to wonder what the judgment does or does not do for you. Write any notes about your discovery here:

_____

_____

_____

_____

Creating Your Own Affirmation Statements

Being able to identify strengths is an important part of being able to use their power to build our confidence and momentum toward change. Being able to recall and notice our strengths helps us connect to the strength and identify as a strong person who has this trait. In motivational interview-ing, such a cohesive observation and reflection on strength is known as an *affirmation statement*. The affirmation calls out your competent behaviors. The affirmation is not hypothetical; it is based on evidence of your effectiveness. The affirmation can also be thought of as a way to bring past strengths–based behavior into the present so these behaviors can be acknowledged again and acted upon for future gain.

Returning to Tegan, let's review how they created two affirmation statements for themself based on their strength identifications:

1.   I am aware that I am intelligent, and I can pay attention. I know this because I have been able to learn two languages and figure out how to succeed in school when the courses were not designed to meet my learning needs.

2.   I notice that I have been courageous my entire life. I know this because I have identified as transgender, and I had to be brave to tell others about my identity when I was not so sure they would support me.

Now it is your turn to create your own affirmation statements. Using the format given, create affirmation statements for yourself based on your strengths. If you need more space to add affirma-tions, go ahead and do that. The more you have, the more confident you will likely be about taking further steps to explore your relationship with substances and take any steps necessary to change. Please feel free to use your own language. The spaces are provided to help guide the exercise, but your natural language is always the best way to explore and express your strengths.

1. I am _____, because _____.

2. I am _____, because _____.

3. I am _____, because _____.

4. I am _____, because _____.

5. I am _____, because _____.

What have you learned about yourself as the result of completing these sentences? How would you describe yourself based on your strengths?

_____

_____

_____

Our self-confidence rises as the result of having and using affirmation statements in our lives. So, what does this mean for exploring areas of change, specifically possibly changing how we relate to substances? The answer to the question is, not surprisingly, highly individualized and quite possibly complicated. At the very least, it is helpful to explore the affirmation statement and consider how being in touch with your strengths and feelings increased confidence, which can function to open up your willingness to explore change options.

Recall that Tegan was oriented toward their family members being the driving force in their recovery. The affirmation list was a way to help them see opportunities for exploring their relationship to cannabis use that they were not open to considering before completing such an exploration. By connecting to their intelligence and courage, Tegan realized that although they liked the way they felt relaxed after smoking cannabis, they were concerned that smoking cannabis was getting in the way of their intellect. When high, they did not want to read, write, or talk about complex things with others. It became clear to Tegan that cannabis was not allowing them to connect to their strengths.

Let's begin exploring how links can be made between your feelings about yourself and the behavioral outcomes you might like to see. The next step is for you to pose a question to consider regarding your relationship with substances. Then you will explore the question in relation to your identified strengths. To give you an idea how to do this, let's look at how Tegan did this exploration.

Tegan had an overarching question: "How can I know for certain that I have an issue with cannabis?" Along with Tegan's lack of self-confidence, their fear about not being able to handle the issues that this question might bring up kept Tegan from exploring their cannabis use. They felt more comfortable avoiding the question. By connecting to their strengths, Tegan knew they had resources to support the exploration. Tegan approached the concern they had about substance use by asking these strengths-based questions.

> How might my **courage** help me address my question? I know I am afraid to think about my cannabis use, but I honestly have been through so much more. Looking at why I smoke cannot be any more fear-provoking than coming out to friends and family.

> How might my **resilience** help me address my question? I have approached a lot of tough things that I had to figure out in the past. Getting through school was really hard for me. I might be uncomfortable if I quit or cut back on cannabis, but it doesn't mean I won't be able to manage. I have honestly had to deal with so much more.

> How might my **honesty** help me address my question? I have been avoiding looking at my cannabis use and this has been a conflict for me because I am an honest person. Avoiding the obvious concerns I have with cannabis does not feel honest to me. I care a lot about not gaslighting myself or others. I think exploring my relationship with cannabis will help me feel a lot better.

> How might my **intelligence** help me address my question? I can thoughtfully use information I read to help me make the best choices about my behavior. I can seek out people who have opinions I trust to help guide me in my exploration, and I can apply the skills I learned in recovery groups before to help me as I start learning more about my relationship with cannabis.

Consider writing a statement for each of your strengths. As you can see in Tegan's exploration around their cannabis use, each strength brings something new to the self-exploration process.

My question to potentially explore about my substance use is: _____

_____

How _____ (enter a strength here) might help me address this question:

_____

_____

How _____ (enter a strength here) might help me address this question:

_____

_____

How _____ (enter a strength here) might help me address this question:

_____

_____

How _____ (enter a strength here) might help me address this question:

_____

_____

As you consider your question, spend a moment taking in all you have learned in your self-exploration process. If you were to pull together the sum of what you have learned about your strengths, what might you include in a paragraph about yourself? As an example, here is Tegan's summary paragraph of their strengths.

I learned that I have much less to fear about exploring my relationship to cannabis. I know I am afraid of having to go through another long and potentially demoralizing rehabilitation program. I am also aware that there is no reason to think that I might have such a terrible experience. I have learned a lot from my earlier experiences that I can apply to my current situation. When I am outmatched, I can step back and listen to good advice. I also know that I can handle looking at how much I smoke, as I have handled so much more in the past. I have demonstrated that I can approach and deal with scary situations, as I have had a life full of scary experiences that I have dealt with on my own. With a strong and loving family by my side, I am willing and open to listen to them and accept their help if I need it and they offer it.

Using Tegan's paragraph as an example, how might you summarize your own strengths? Write your summary paragraph here:

_____

_____

_____

_____

_____

_____

_____

_____

_____

Now that you have summarized your experiences exploring your strengths via affirmation statements, what do you think you'll do next? This question naturally evokes our interest in and willingness to change. This will be the topic of the next chapter where we ask ourselves the important questions about what we care about and consider how we might act on our values in order to move toward change.

CHAPTER 7

Gather Support from Others

When seeking treatment for substance use in the past, you may have faced distrust and suspicion from treatment providers. There is a natural ambivalence that occurs as the result of trying to pull away from a substance. Because the substance has hijacked our executive functioning and created a powerful reinforcement through increase in pleasure and reduction of pain, our words and actions are often perceived as dishonest or "manipulation" by people trying to help. As a result, the power in the relationship has often shifted to the helper (for example, a counselor or sponsor), who is seen as essential in guiding us to abstinence (Miller, Forcehimes, and Zweben 2019). But when we are not seen as the experts on ourselves, we might not want to participate, as we do not have control over what we are doing in our recovery work. This lack of control can be highly stressful and even cause us to leave treatment.

You likely want to feel heard. You may want someone to collaborate with you. This is why motivational interviewing has historically shifted the power dynamic from the professional leading and directing the change process to a more collaborative process between the provider and the person seeking help. This cooperation enables you to come up with your own solutions while being supported by a helper who can humbly provide guidance without trying to determine the agenda or overcontrol the outcome (Miller and Rollnick 2023).

When you work with a counselor, the goal of your partnership with them is to promote safety and guidance toward change. When you explore a relationship with substances independently, creating partnerships is also important. By reading this book, you are already engaged in an independent activity to explore your relationship with substances. This workbook exploration is also a form of partnership. Collaboration is the most direct way to gain support and potential guidance in the process of self-exploration.

You might be using this book because you do not have many people you trust to share your concerns. Or you might have many family members, colleagues, or friends who would be open to supporting you on almost any aspect of self-growth. Most of us are somewhere in between these extremes. We all have a different level of comfort between complete openness and being more guarded. Fortunately, feeling connected and being part of a group requires that we have just one other person to collaborate with (Lynch 2018).

When Craig was asked to consider who would support him and help him think through his next steps in recovery, his friend Jeff seemed like the obvious choice. He could have considered other possible resources such as a family member, a close and trusted work colleague, a 12-step or other program sponsor, a faith leader or member of his church, or even a support group. Supporters can be anyone who is present, willing, and able to be in relationship with us. It's important to find someone who can both help support a conversation about change without having to control the conversation and whose presence is so comforting that we feel fully safe to be who we are. This enables us to be open and available to explore our experiences, needs, and next steps.

Using the following table, consider who you might choose to be your recovery support and why. How might you approach them about your relationship to substances? Try to consider as many people as possible, but know you can have some wonderful partnering with even one person.

Name of support person	How might they be helpful in my exploration?	What can I offer this person in return?	Examples of how I might ask them to support me
Craig's example: Jeff	Jeff seems to be able to notice when I am upset, even before I notice I am upset. He seems comfortable communicating with me, and he seems to want to help.	I can be sure that I listen to Jeff at times when he needs support as well.	I might tell him that I have appreciated his comments in the past. I can ask if he might be comfortable continuing to let me know if I seem to be struggling with my emotions or behaviors.

When thinking about who you might have for support, it is likely you are thinking about various individuals in your life. Although it can be difficult to identify even one person with whom you can connect and create a trusting relationship, doing so is essential for change. You might also be concerned that you just do not have a support system of people who understand your journey through substance use. This might be the case if you have family members and friends who also use substances. They might even feel threatened or vulnerable, as looking at your own use might compel them to consider their own connection to substances. Such a situation is not uncommon, which is why many people choose to find professionals and peers, groups, and organizations that promote themselves as being open to having conversations about substance use and change. Many programs are free or low fee, and confidentiality or anonymity is part of most programming.

Supportive Resources Available to You

Although the following is not an exhaustive list, it provides information on organizations that are willing to have conversations with you about your substance use. The government agencies base their information on scientific research and existing substance use treatment policy.

Twelve-step programming: Twelve-step and other support groups have their own philosophy on how people heal. It is based on a spiritual program that promotes fellowship among participants. They promote abstinence (no substance use at all) and the group materials, programming, and practices are based on assumptions that attendees will move toward quitting all substances. Twelve-step programming does function as harm-reduction in practice, as those attending the meetings will be allowed to keep attending even if they return to use. Many people considering recovery found 12-step to be essential to learning about themselves and the options around substance use treatment.

Other support groups: Some support groups are not 12-step based, such as LifeRing, and Secular Organizations for Sobriety (SOS). These programs are mostly based on offering you cognitive and behavioral skills to assist with problem solving. They support people who do not want to return to using substances.

Treatment programs: Treatment programs are typically residential programs where people live or attend programming during the day. They can offer you more intensive support while you stop using substances and obtain large amounts of individual and group support in order to learn to approach life without substances. Residential treatment is typically used by and recommended for people who need extra support to abstain from using while withdrawing from substances and learning how to avoid relapsing on alcohol or drugs.

Other resources: In the Resources section at the back of this book, I offer some websites and numbers to get you started exploring the private and discreet services offered to support you. The resources listed in the back of the book are free or request donation only. Those programs with meetings have meetings online and many have meetings in person. Although the list is not comprehensive, it has many accessible resources that can be used at virtually any time. Even if you are considering change but are not quite there yet, you will find that many people who have learned about their substance use benefitted from going to meetings and learning from the wealth of wisdom in the various meetings. Flynn serves as an example of how meetings might be used:

★ Flynn's Story

Flynn had been smoking cocaine for eight months. He became concerned about his substance use after he was arrested for possession following a traffic stop. Flynn has a job as a project manager for a tech firm and is married to his partner. The arrest and resulting probation sentencing have caused Flynn to worry about his future and the possibility of losing those things most important to him: his relationship, his livelihood, and the respect of his family.

Not sure what he should do, Flynn attended a Narcotics Anonymous meeting because he had a college friend who attended NA. Flynn participated in the meeting online, and he was too embarrassed to turn on his camera. He sat and listened, wondering if he was like everyone else in the room. He found that he did not think his situation was as extreme as some of the speakers who shared how far they tumbled before they stopped using. However, Flynn did identify with some of the speakers who had similar backgrounds and grew up in the same community. Flynn left the meeting not entirely sure if he would attend again, but he did learn how people came to understand when they had a problem with a substance, and he found himself moved by what they shared with the group and how sincere and real they appeared to be.

Choose an organization from the list in the Resources section at the back of this book (or elsewhere) to explore. After reviewing their resources online or perhaps by attending a meeting, consider how this organization could be useful in your own exploration of your substance use. Write down your thoughts:

_____

_____

_____

_____

_____

Managing Support from Others

As we discussed, people who use substances face discrimination and stigma that might result in their holding back and declining to reach out to others for support. It is hard to know how many people cannot get the support they need from others because of this understandable reluctance to share information that makes them vulnerable. But you might have noticed that among the people who want to help you, many are often very eager to show support. Whether as an attendee in a group or as a coworker, family member, or friend, many people want to step up and be helpful. This willingness to be a support is wonderful—until it isn't.

You might have noticed that well-intentioned people who want to help can be very active in trying to fix the problem. It makes sense. We fix leaks in our roofs, we patch tires, and change dirty diapers. Humans are amazing at fixing things—except at fixing other humans.

Through your work in chapter 6, you have learned how to perceive your strengths and abilities to power your change. When well-intentioned people tell you how to change your life, you likely feel disempowered as they (often unintentionally) ignore what you have already done to take care of yourself. Because you need to remain empowered in order to move your change agenda forward, it is important for you to find ways of managing, to the best of your ability, how you receive advice and guidance from others.

Here are some ways you can be open to receive help while also remaining in charge of how you take in and manage the support you receive:

State what you've tried when asking for advice or guidance: State what you have already tried and think about what kind of help you would like, before you ask for help. Doing such preparation will help the people you ask know what kind of information you would like and what would be helpful for you.

Choose between multiple options: If you want advice, tell people who might be supportive that you would like advice and you would like to be able to choose among different options. We are more likely to select advice when we have more than one piece of advice from which to choose. Get second and third opinions. Although it can take a bit more time, the more information you get from a number of people, the more options you will have to help inform the choices you would like to make.

Be aware of their motivations to persuade you: When someone has agreed to support you, notice if you feel that they might be trying to persuade you to make a particular decision regarding your substance use concern. You might have a close relationship with this person, and you might, for any number of reasons, not want to directly confront them. However, being aware that they have a perspective they are trying to promote can help you understand how their point of view is influencing you.

Know when you can trust: Trust those people who show they listen to you, are open to your point of view, and have your best interests at heart. Trust those people who want to help you reduce your pain and suffering, and who support your choices on how you would like to address your substance use.

★ Tina's Story

Tina had been questioning her cocaine use for several months. What had seemed to her a reasonable drug to socialize with every few weeks became increasingly concerning to Tina. She was not concerned about her ability to stop if she wanted to stop using. She was more concerned about other substances that might be present in the drug, as she had been hearing about cocaine being cut with fentanyl. She was growing more concerned about possible unintentional overdoses. She brought this concern up with her friends, and one told her not to worry as he was buying from a "safe source." Another friend implied that she might be a bit paranoid. Tina did not want to risk her friendships, but she was becoming increasingly concerned with ongoing news reports. She did learn from conversations with her friends that they did not seem to know, and maybe did not want to know, about dangers of drugs cut with fentanyl.

Tina became clear that knowing more about the public health issue was very important to her. She chose to contact the SAMHSA (Substance Abuse and Mental Health Services Administration) Helpline, which put her in contact with a number of harm-reduction providers who could help answer her questions privately and without judgment. What Tina discovered is that recreational drugs can be tested for the presence of fentanyl. Tina appreciated knowing that such resources exist and that she had the choice to purchase drug testing strips if she chose to use cocaine in the future. Being able to ask about her concerns without having a pro- or anti-drug agenda was a relief to Tina. In addition to being able to make better choices for herself, she found that she was able to increase her trust in others and was more willing to ask questions in the future.

Exploring your use of substances can be overwhelming and anxiety provoking. You might be worried about judgment from others or suspicious of others' motives. How any one group or program talks about the issue of substance use might not fit for you or your cultural background. The good news is that there are many options for effective, science-based, supportive guidance. There are also options that focus on spirituality and values. Some resources can be used in the privacy of your home, and others promote the power of community and fellowship to foster growth and understanding. So many options exist that it is highly likely that with a little exploration, and some help from your friends (and soon-to-be friends), you will find a path that works for you. As you gain more support and clarity on the facts and what you need, you will likely become increasingly ready to explore your substance use more deeply and meaningfully. Opening yourself up to the big questions could lead you on a path to change. In the next chapter, you will further explore what your current substance use means to you and what may or may not be important as you consider change. This exploration will occur as you practice asking yourself questions designed to help you explore what is important and meaningful to you.

CHAPTER 8

Dive into the Big Questions

Are you ready to dive into the big questions that will help you to think about your current situation and identify what change you might consider? If so, you are ready for some evocative conversations. As you've done in earlier chapters, you will explore these questions by responding to writing prompts or questions. In motivational interviewing, the *evocation* process is based on an expectation that you are open to change and are willing to talk about your current situation and potentially new behavior. The power of evocation is based on the fact that you are more likely to talk yourself into change *when you hear what you are saying out loud.*

Think of a time when you thought, *I can't believe I am saying that.* Such recognition is an example of the power of evocation. Thoughts can bounce around in your head in a way that enables you to ruminate in endless loops and talk yourself further into stuck places. On the other hand, if you open up your thoughts and set them free so you can hear them and others can respond to them, your awareness increases. You become aware of those thoughts about what you are doing, what you need, and what next steps you might consider on the path to change.

In the tradition of self-improvement and recovery, evocation and increased awareness comes in many forms: support groups, fellowships, meditation groups, journaling. In motivational interviewing, evocation is also an opportunity to notice and respond to *change talk.* Change talk is any articulation of a change in behavior that will move you through your current concerns (the focus of our next chapter). In the case of substance use concerns, the change you're exploring is moving away from a current practice of substance use and moving toward cutting back or abstaining. Evocation serves as an excellent opportunity for examining your current life situation. Asking yourself *How is this working out for me?* is a significant step toward exploring possibilities of change.

The Open-Ended Question

One of the skills used to promote evocation is the open-ended question. The open-ended question is one in which the answer does not typically generate a short response statement. It is different from the closed question (for example, "What color is your hair?"), which is offered in order to obtain a specific answer (Miller and Rollnick 2023). An example of an open-ended question would be "Can you tell me a bit about your favorite hobbies?" or "Tell me a bit about your favorite hobbies." While not always phrased as a question, the "tell me" type of leading invitation also tends to bring forth a narrative. In response to these invitations, it would be hard to imagine someone just stating, "I like building guitars and being part of a synchronized swim team." It is possible that someone could list hobbies in response, but doing so is highly unlikely. It's much more likely a story will emerge because open-ended questions are not asking for a list; they are asking for a description. Consider Gene's response to this evocation.

★ Gene's Story

I have always loved playing guitars. In high school, I was in a band, and I wanted a certain sound, so I started to experiment with putting together different types of guitars using kits and then eventually started to learn how to build my own from scratch. Later in life, I was fortunate enough to have a daughter. She was diagnosed with rheumatoid arthritis as a child. When her physician recommended she take up swimming, I joined her so we could spend more time together. One summer she begged to take a synchronized swimming class as she was getting so bored with lap swimming. I thought, *Why not? She's my kid.* I see dads dress up for tea parties, so what the hell. I loved it. She liked it, but gradually took up other hobbies. I continued with a men's team, and I am now part of the Floating Blokes swim group. I love the practice as it's a tough workout, and the other guys don't take themselves too seriously.

What images came to mind as you read that paragraph? It is reasonable to assume that Gene is curious and open. He starts learning something, and then he finds himself engaged in the hobby. He is willing to try new hobbies that might not be common, such as building guitars, and not "typical" for his gender, such as synchronized swimming. He also appears to be someone who develops and builds relationships with others; we know he has been a band member, an engaged and supportive father, and a positive teammate. It is likely you have noticed some other potential qualities as a picture of this individual develops.

A good open-ended question does not reveal everything we need to know about someone, and the answers are open to our own interpretation. Having a conversation that enables us to learn about others or ourselves is important. The following questions are designed to evoke some ideas you might have about your own relationship to substances. Choose some or all of the questions to answer, and then consider the response that the question evoked from you: What does this response tell you about yourself? What does your answer tell you about the possible next steps you might take regarding your own relationship to substances?

What Is Your Relationship to Substances?

By asking these "big" questions, you can talk through your own reasons for change and to discover what it might mean for you to do something different in your current life situation. You might want to read through the questions first and then decide which questions mean the most to you. Choose as many to respond to as you like. Everyone who is asked these questions will have their own unique answers. Write your answers to the questions in the spaces provided.

What are the most important reasons for you to explore your relationship to substances?

1. _____

2. _____

3. _____

4. _____

5. _____

What does it mean to "change your relationship to substances"?

_____

_____

_____

_____

_____

It is likely that the substances you have used helped you in some way. How have your substances helped you?

_____

_____

_____

_____

If you did change your substance use behavior, what other tools might you use to help you cope? For instance, if you were using alcohol to deal with social discomfort, what else might you consider doing to help you cope with being around people?

_____

_____

_____

_____

_____

If you were to change your relationship to substances, how might you live your life differently?

_____

_____

_____

_____

_____

If you were to change your relationship to substances, how might you think differently about yourself?

_____

_____

_____

_____

_____

What other changes have you made in your life that would help you now as you consider changing your relationship to substances?

_____

_____

_____

_____

_____

_____

_____

What Might Your Next Steps Be?

Read through each of your responses in the previous section. Do you have any thoughts about what steps you might take in addressing your substance use? What might such thoughts be? Reflect on them with the following prompts.

What, if anything, are you considering changing?

_____

_____

_____

_____

_____

After considering your answers to this question, what else do you need to explore (for example, people who can help, decisions that need to be made, or resources you might need)?

_____

_____

_____

_____

_____

These questions probably generated some new ideas for you to consider. Each question was written in a way to help you come up with ideas to move from where you are now—considering exploring your relationship to substances—to taking the next steps in determining how substances are impacting you right now and how they might potentially impact you in the future.

Review your responses to all the questions you have answered so far in this chapter. Although this list of questions is not exhaustive, you likely learned something about yourself and your relationship to substances. You might have come up with some desires, reasons, or needs to make changes in your life. You might have even considered some steps that you might take toward the life you want to have. In the next chapter, you will begin to identify change talk. You can come back to your answers to these questions when you start to use your own change talk to build your change plan.

As you responded to the questions, you might have noticed ways in which asking yourself questions versus reflecting on your own thoughts and feelings (as you did in chapter 5) feels different.

Here, write the ways in which asking questions of yourself feels different than reflecting on your feelings and thoughts. Can one, the other, or both styles of inquiry help you learn about yourself and what you need and want as you consider your next steps toward change?

_____

_____

_____

_____

Earlier we met Craig, who was struggling with self-compassion. He also chose to be curious about his relationship to alcohol. When Craig faced these questions about his relationship to substances and what his next steps might be, he intended to complete all the questions from beginning to end. Instead, he read through them first and chose to start with this question: "If you were to change your relationship to substances, how might you feel differently about yourself?"

Craig was struck by this particular question, as he had already explored how hard he had been on himself while considering the topic of self-compassion. He thought maybe exploring the impact drinking has on his self-perception was a good idea. He also read through the other questions just in case this question was not the best one to start with at this time. He felt the pull to explore this issue, which is important as he wanted to spend his time well learning about himself and why he was so stuck on drinking. Craig wrote the following in response to the question he chose to focus on:

> I feel as if I hate myself every day when I drink. I go to a party and start out feeling pretty good, but when I am around other people and meeting new men, I just cannot stand the discomfort. I find myself having a drink to relax and try to fit in, but then I notice I have another drink, and after about the third—I need to be honest here—I lose self-control. It is losing my self-control that I find so shameful. I always tell myself it is going to be different this time. I can stop at two. I never stop at two, and usually I can remember past three drinks. If I was able to control my drinking, if I *can* control my drinking, I would not hate myself so much.

After rereading the question and considering his relationship to alcohol, Craig delved a bit more into his thoughts:

I clearly cannot control my drinking. I really want to control my drinking. Can I maybe learn how to do this? I am not sure. Ten or even five years ago, my losing control when I drank just did not seem to be a problem. I have some friends who end up pretty sloppy, and I don't want to be like them. I know other people laugh at them, and I don't want to be laughed at like that. It is humiliating. Being laughed at because I am drunk is my greatest fear.

When the third prompt asked Craig to consider if he might do anything with his new awareness, he wrote:

I am not entirely certain where to start. I do know that I don't want to completely quit drinking yet—that is a big move. I have a couple of friends who stopped drinking. I would like to talk to them about what they did to manage their alcohol. I am a bit concerned, as I don't want them trying to influence me or tell me what to do. I suppose I am my own person. I just want to know what they did so I can learn more about the impact of their alcohol use and the choices they could make.

Finally, Craig looked at what resources he might explore:

One thing I could do, that no one would have to know about, is I could go online and research alcohol use. I am not exactly sure where to start, but I think I will look at medical sites. I also know there are apps that friends have downloaded, and I wonder if any of those apps are really good. I could check them out, as most of them should have free versions. I like the idea of doing some research before talking to anyone. I do feel embarrassed, and I don't want to be any more vulnerable by asking for help. I know I might eventually ask for help, but I want some answers first. I would like to hear what is recommended and get some more facts about alcohol.

Now that you have had an opportunity to ask yourself some of these "big" questions and have read about Craig's experience, take time to consider how the answers to your questions are coming together for you. Review your responses to the prompts as a way to bring together what you have learned about yourself.

Big Questions Sometimes Generate More Questions

The answers to big questions might seem overwhelming, and they're certainly not tidy. You will likely find that big questions end up leading to more questions, and that can seem confusing. The point of questions is that they help you explore your internal world. It is likely that you have many thoughts and feelings that lead to behaviors, which in turn result in more thinking and feeling. All of this is normal, and thoughtful questions can help you identify new themes. More important, the act of questioning can help you step back and observe your answers, which quite often results in important themes and potentially some *aha!* moments. You can start to notice how what you do, think, and feel as the result of your substance use impacts what you care about and what you want in life.

What Are Your New Questions?

It does not mean you are stuck if you find yourself wondering about your next move. Write down some of the new questions you have here. These questions might lead to other important places to explore as you move toward additional self-reflection or planning your next steps.

_____

_____

_____

_____

_____

_____

What Surprised You About Yourself?

Did you learn something new about yourself? Did you become aware of some idea about yourself that, at one time, did not seem that important, but it seems important now? Write about it.

_____

_____

_____

_____

_____

_____

_____

You might notice that you have some new knowledge, or point of view, about yourself that you did not have when you started this chapter. Although change can seem overwhelming and difficult, your changing thoughts about yourself and your own personal story with substances is important. It is likely you will start thinking differently about yourself before you start to make the changes you want. You will use what you learned in this chapter to help you create your path for change in chapter 9. So keep this chapter close, because you will be using it to lay the foundations for your pathway for change.

Focus Your Attention on Change

Having a conversation about change sounds simple enough. But what does it mean to have a meaningful conversation about change that actually translates into change in behavior? It is not uncommon to hear the expression "talking the talk" about something we want to change, but it is quite another matter to actually "walk the walk." If it were easy to make that change, most of us would have already made any number of changes in our lives! This chapter will help you understand what change talk is, how to recognize it in yourself, and how to work with it so that it motivates you to change your actions.

What Is Change Talk, Exactly?

Change talk is any verbalization that moves from the status quo of any selected target behavior toward any stated interest or intent to do something different. For example, change talk about my drinking or other substance use might sound like "I'd like to cut back" or "Maybe I'll learn more about the effects of substances on the body." In motivational interviewing, practitioners intentionally seek out and reinforce change talk as it appears. Thinking and writing about the need, desire, reason, or importance of change helps build momentum toward change talk that mobilizes us to consider change, commit to change, or take steps toward a change goal. Change talk is considered a distinct feature of motivational interviewing, and clinicians who use it generate change talk and reinforce it when it occurs (Miller and Rollnick 2023). In this chapter, you will learn to identify your own change talk and build it up to promote change for yourself.

The first step in generating your motivational change talk is becoming aware of your own change conversations. Like all of us, you undoubtedly have conversations with yourself about your day, your relationships with others, and your dilemmas or problems. In these internal conversations, it's likely you are speaking to some component of change: why you might need to change, what it would be like for you to change, and why you would want to change, among other ideas. Because it is likely that you are already having change conversations, you just need to shift your attention to these internal dialogues and notice how you might build and strengthen such ideas. Just as we can find ways to manage our self-talk, such as the negative things we say to ourselves, we can also find ways to promote language that empowers us and moves us toward making different choices and shifting our behaviors in positive ways.

When you move away from your current situation and toward change, you might notice that the change talk in your thoughts or with others could be considered either *preparatory* or *mobilizing* change talk. They function differently in the ways they promote change (Miller and Rollnick 2023). Specifically, the change talk can either *prepare* you to change or *mobilize* you to engage in the change process.

Preparatory Change Talk

Preparatory change talk typically occurs early in a conversation or a session with a therapist. It is characterized by statements in which you talk about your reasons, wants, abilities, and desires to change. You might speak to many aspects of desire, reason, or importance regarding change early and often in the process.

Sometimes, you might even feel frustrated when you hear yourself speaking a lot of preparatory change talk. This frustration comes from listening to yourself come up with compelling ideas regarding how you can or should change, but then you do not do it. Even professionals become annoyed when they work with someone who speaks of change because they interpret this change talk as a sign that the person will immediately take the next step to change—but then they don't. The good news is, this is not a time to get frustrated. Why? Because this early change talk is, in fact, change!

If you talk about your reasons, desires, needs, and wants around change, that is a type of change. It is changing your thoughts, and the more you attend to all the reasons, needs, desires, and wants, the more you build momentum toward actually carrying out the change. Take Sandy as an example.

★ Sandy's Story

Sandy has been thinking about her relationship to vaping cannabis for a couple of years. Sandy has not stopped or even slowed down her use, but her thoughts are changing. Five years ago, Sandy enjoyed vaping cannabis at least twice a day. She found it relaxing at night, and during the day Sandy experienced less anxiety. Recently, though, Sandy has been engaged in thinking and talking about vaping, becoming curious about how it is affecting her life. She feels clarity when she identifies each component of change talk in conversations with herself and others.

Preparatory change talk typically verbalizes one of four things: desire, ability, reason, or need. Each one is important to explore, as each has the ability to build motivational momentum toward change.

Desire: A desire refers to what you want to change. Sandy may *want* to explore her relationship to cannabis as she values being a good role model for her daughter. Her change talk might sound something like, "I did not have great parental role models growing up, and it is *important to me* that I address my own issues with cannabis so my daughter can see how grown-ups deal with the world and make better choices." Here the words "important to me" indicate her desire to change.

Read through your responses to the evocative questions in chapter 8 to identify the things you *want or desire* to change. Consider starting your sentences with "I want…" or "I would like…" as a way to focus on what you want in changing your substance use. Sandy might write, *I want to cut back on vaping, so I can be a better role model for my kids.*

I want _____

_____.

I want _____

_____.

I would like _____

_____.

I would like_____

_____.

Ability: This relates to the perceived confidence you have regarding your capacity to make a change. When you feel able, you recognize that you have the skills and knowledge about what you need to do for change. You also have the perceived or actual ability to make the change. Such confidence in ability is important, as lack of skill or confidence is a major reason behavior change does not happen. Without the ability that comes from experience and skills, you could be setting yourself up for failure. The good news is that you can build skills that enable you to reach your goals.

As Sandy wrote, *I stopped drinking when I was pregnant and at other times in my life when I knew I just did not want to drink anymore. I know being there for my daughter is important, and I can stop using cannabis when I am ready.* Her ability to stop is highlighted here in the statement, "I can stop using cannabis." Change talk is expressed in the present and future tenses. If someone changed in the past, that is not considered change talk. However, your past success at change can be helpful for forming current change talk; what you did in the past to address your challenges might be useful in the present as you make your current change.

For instance, if you were able to quit smoking cigarettes for six months, you were making decisions and behaving in ways that demonstrated your ability to quit smoking. It is quite possible you were able to find a way to manage cravings. Maybe you were able to avoid being around others when they were smoking, thus avoiding being tempted to smoke when you saw them light up. If these are behaviors you had in the past that helped you change behavior, you may be able to do them again.

Consider what you learned and wrote about yourself in chapter 8. Read through your responses and write about your *ability* to change. You might want to consider starting with, "I can…" or "I am able to…" statements. For instance, *I am able to ask for support when I find myself craving a drink.*

I can _____

_____.

I can _____

_____.

I am able to _____

_____.

I am able to _____

_____.

Reason: A reason to change is any fact that makes you want to alter the current situation. A reason can be thought of (or stated as) an "if...then" proposition. For example, Sandy might realize, "If I continue to smoke cannabis daily, then I will have difficulty paying my rent." Her reason for questioning her cannabis use may or may not be a significant reason for someone else to change. In your case, all that matters is that whatever reasons you choose to change are important reasons for you.

Consider what you learned about yourself from the evocative questions in chapter 8. What are reasons for you to change? It helps to write "If..., then..." statements. For example, *If I cut back on how much cocaine I use, then my friends will not be as worried about my health.* Another way of creating reasons to change is to consider what you do not want to happen as the result of your substance use. For instance, *I do not want to keep spending so much money on alcohol.* You can start with "I do not want to..." and then express your reason for change.

If _____,

then _____.

If _____,

then _____.

I do not want to _____

_____.

I do not want to _____

_____.

Need: A need for change indicates an urgency or a requirement for change. It is typically a more motivating factor pushing change. A need might be indicated by language such as "I have to..." or "I must..." followed by the change. It is common to have a stated need occur along with a more passionate or emotional response. Sandy might bring up her own need to change in a statement such as, *I have to cut back on my vaping. My daughter is only eight, and last night she said that I ignore her after I have been vaping for a while.*

Considering your thoughts about your substance use so far, what need do you have to change your use? It can help to complete this sentence: *When it comes to using…, I need to….* For example, the sentence can state, *When it comes to using unprescribed stimulates to stay focused, I must find out if it is safe or if it is putting me at risk of harm.*

When it comes to using _____,

I need to _____.

When it comes to using _____,

I need to _____.

When it comes to using _____,

I need to _____.

When it comes to using _____,

I need to _____.

Collect Your DARN Change Talk

Let's deepen clarity on what your unique change talk is. Take a look at your exercise responses in chapter 5, when you reflected on your experience with substances. Read through your answers, and circle or highlight any desire, ability, reason, need (DARN) change talk. You might not find all of the DARN change talk when you read through the exercises, as it can be embedded in various statements that make it hard to identify. That's okay. Consider returning to the exercise in a couple of days and going through it again. Did you find more DARN change talk?

Write the change talk sentences (or parts of sentences) that you discovered as you read your exercise responses in chapter 5:

_____

_____

_____

_____

_____

_____

_____

_____

_____

_____

What impact does reading your change talk have on you when you see all these statements together?

_____

_____

_____

Were you surprised by any of your change talk?

_____

_____

Now that you see the change statements together, what do you think you will do next?

_____

_____

_____

_____

_____

_____

Mobilizing Change Talk

Your answer to the last question may have led you to think about action steps toward change. When we think about all the benefits of changing as well as all the problems with *not* changing, we are likely more compelled to make a move toward change. Such an action move might be a very small one, but many larger changes in life are propelled forward by smaller steps. We will now explore several types of mobilizing change talk, such as commitment, activation, and taking steps.

Commitment

Mobilizing change talk includes any language that indicates you are committed to change. Examples would be "I will go to a 12-step meeting on Thursday" or "I will talk to my doctor about getting a patch to help with nicotine withdrawal." Commitment statements are change talk because they specifically state an intent to act: "I will," "I must," "I am going to."

The commitment statement is a clear move away from your current situation toward change. It indicates that you may be ready to move from commitment to action planning. In fact, if you are especially eager to get a solid commitment statement—from yourself or others—you might overlook other types of change talk. So, although commitment language is welcome and serves an important purpose in building your momentum toward change, be sure to not lose sight of the other components of mobilizing change talk that can help build a path toward commitment. An initial commitment to taking the first step toward change is how the change process begins.

> Sandy spent a significant amount of time considering how her relationship to cannabis impacted her need to save money, be a good role model, and engage more in life. After several months of consideration, she decided she was willing to make a commitment to cut back on vaping. She was not sure if she was ready to stop cannabis entirely, but she wanted to at least cut back so she could see if it made any difference in her mood and ability to focus on activities she was trying to complete. She noticed she was willing to state, "I will cut back to using cannabis no more than three times on the weekend." Sandy could decide to cut back more or less after she tries to stop using, but here she is on her path to initiating a change.

Given that everyone is motivated to change or do something, write down action(s) that you are committed to taking in your life. It does not have to be related to substance use. It might be a mundane action that you do daily, but which you are committed to doing. This could include taking a quick walk during lunch or stretching at least three times a day. Feel free to write in all the activities you are committed to completing on a regular basis:

I will _____

_____

I must _____

_____

I am going to _____

_____

Review the list. Notice what comes up for you when you take inventory of all the change you regularly commit to completing. Recognize that there are days when we succeed in change and days when we do not. When you review all the changes you regularly sign on to complete in your day-to-day life, what comes to mind? Write what you notice here:

_____

_____

_____

_____

_____

Now notice when in your life you were able to complete these commitments. What was occurring in your life that made it possible for you to complete these commitments?

_____

_____

_____

How were you able to establish your commitments?

_____

_____

_____

Which were easy to accomplish?

_____

_____

_____

Which were harder to start or complete?

_____

_____

_____

How did you go about creating your intention and following through on it?

_____

_____

_____

_____

Were some commitments easier to establish than others?

_____

_____

_____

As you write about your change process, notice how you initiate, build, and sustain commitment to change. As you make a commitment to change, you might notice a pattern to your process. For instance, you might notice that when you do activities with others, such as going to a meeting or an exercise class, you are more likely to follow through on completing them. When you notice this pattern, it will probably also help you to explore your relationship to substances and choose your first steps toward change. Write here what you noticed about how you commit.

_____

_____

_____

_____

_____

Activation

Activation talk is another form of mobilizing change talk. Activation change talk is commonly seen as tentative—*maybe* or *perhaps* you will take a step toward change. Examples of activation talk include statements such as "I'll consider talking to someone about being my sponsor" or "Perhaps I will cut back one drink a day." You may ignore your activation change talk or not take it seriously, because it often includes statements made when you are on a path toward change but have not fully committed to that change.

Activation change talk provides an excellent opportunity to see the glass half full instead of half empty. When you state that you might cut back on smoking, you are indicating a willingness to change your relationship to the substance. If you focus only on the fact that you are not completely committed to quitting, that might be seeing the glass as half empty. However, if you focus on the fact that you are open to cutting back, as indicated by the word "might," you are focusing on what is possible and seeing the glass as half full. When you only see progress toward change expressed in solid commitment statements, you are missing an opportunity to build on the little steps that tilt toward change. A statement that indicates you just might consider attending a "sober curious" nonalcohol party is a movement toward, rather than away from, commitment.

A nonactivation statement would include things like "I could never imagine going to a party without booze" (which supports the current situation that includes drinking to socialize) or "A sober curious party could be a good move for someone who doesn't want to drink, but it's really not for me" (which indicates the speaker sees themself as an exception). Compare those nonactivation statements to those that do indicate some energy toward change, even if they do not reveal full commitment. "I would consider going to a sober curious party if I had someone to go with me" (the conditional aspect indicates they might be committed with support). "Perhaps a sober curious party would be just as fun as one in which everyone is getting loaded, especially later in the evening" (they recognize the benefits of such an event).

As these examples demonstrate, activation has energy or momentum toward change. A liberating aspect of activation language is its ability to help free you up to consider possibilities. Commitment language clearly builds momentum toward creating firm goals, whereas activation language can be used to help you consider experimenting with and trying out change. An experiment, which might be phrased as an opportunity to try out a new activity, is a type of commitment—albeit framed as not necessarily leading to a fuller commitment. The experiment is designed as a learning exercise you might engage or make different choices to promote change.

Therefore, activation statements are ripe for potential experimentation. For example, the statement, "Maybe a sober curious party would be kind of fun to check out. I wonder who would be there." The "maybe" phrasing indicates an openness to the idea of checking out a sober curious party.

Consider your response to a simple evocative question to explore willingness: "What might need to happen for you to check out a sober curious party?"

_____

_____

_____

Possible answers for this example could include "I think I would go if I knew who was throwing the party" or "I might go if I had someone to come with me."

Now consider this: "Imagine you were at a sober curious party. What do you think got you to go?"

_____

_____

_____

A possible answer for this question might be "I got here because I had time, I found a party that fit my schedule, and it is near my house."

Notice that each of these questions helps generate answers that could potentially form the basis of an experiment: "I'll check it out and see how it goes" or "I want to attend sober curious parties to learn more about options to not drink" (an actual commitment to change).

Sandy is not sure she wants to attend a 12-step meeting to support parents abstaining from drugs. She does not know if she wants to stop using cannabis entirely, and she has some fear that she will be judged for smoking cannabis at home, around her children, if she goes to a parental support meeting. A friend strongly encourages Sandy to try it out to see if she likes it, and Sandy tells her friend she will think about attending. She remains concerned about possibly being judged, but she also thinks that her life is really no one else's business and she has every right to see if the meeting would be helpful for her. Sandy tells her friend, "Well, maybe I will think about going..."

Sandy is not fully committed, but she is leaning in a direction toward change, and that is important. As in Sandy's example, the open ambivalence of the activation statement is likely familiar to you. Before you fully commit to an action, it makes sense that you explore and consider the pathways to change. How could you possibly know what to commit to without some curiosity and openness to the options?

Consider at least three things in your life that you are thinking about maybe, possibly, perhaps doing. The activities do not have to relate to substance use; they can be anything you might be open to trying. List them here:

_____

_____

_____

_____

_____

How many items did you notice you were willing to try? Were you surprised by the number of potential opportunities you have to explore something new? Choose one of the activities. Write an activation statement about the activity. Examples might include "I would consider stopping cannabis if I had something to help manage my pain" or "Maybe I will check out an online support group for women who want to discuss their relationships to substances."

My activation statement:

_____

_____

Once you have your statement, ask yourself the following questions regarding your activation statement:

What do I need in order to commit to this activity?

_____

_____

_____

If I imagine having done this, what might have helped me move from considering doing this to actually doing it?

_____

_____

_____

_____

_____

What are some good reasons for doing this?

_____

_____

_____

_____

If anything shifted for you as a result of asking these questions, write down what shifted for you.

_____

_____

_____

_____

_____

_____

_____

_____

_____

_____

_____

Taking Steps

Taking steps is a particularly satisfying type of change talk, as it acknowledges that movement is being made toward a goal or final destination. When you talk about taking steps toward a goal, you are indicating how you already are participating in active behavior change, even though it may not be the behavior initially targeted for change. An example of how taking steps emerges as a form of change talk occurs when Sandy speaks about attending a 12-step meeting to learn about recovery, and she states she was able to obtain the meeting schedules. She has not gone to a meeting yet, but she has completed an initial first step toward meeting attendance by finding where and when the meetings are held.

This is often the first move you can take to support your recovery. If you are considering behavior change, giving up or significantly altering a behavior can be overwhelming. In fact, the looming nature of behavior change can result in mentally checking out, or other avoidance strategies, that keep you from making the first important moves toward change. Taking steps, including very small steps, is often key in initiating and sustaining the momentum needed to follow through on change goals. The small steps that help create a pathway toward change can be thought of as rungs on a ladder. The farther apart each rung, the more difficult it will be to climb the ladder. You can imagine that each step you take on the path to change is like setting the rungs of the ladder closer together. With closer rungs, climbing the ladder is not as much of a stretch because each rung gradually moves you toward the prize.

It is quite likely that you have already had experiences of breaking down goals into smaller steps. "Chunking" components of an assignment to complete in order to make a deadline is a common practice among successful students and creative types who are expected to deliver on deadline. Sometimes you have no idea where to start on a large project and taking a first step—any step—can help disrupt inertia or avoidance that can keep you stuck.

Consider a goal you have. It can be big or small. It might not be directly related to your substance use. Later in this book, we will explore how to make relevant goals more specific so they can be more easily achieved. In this exercise, you will just practice how to break down your goals. The intention is to help you develop the ability to notice where initial steps can be taken. The ability to break apart steps to goals can help increase confidence in approaching larger tasks. It might be helpful to remember that you are practicing making the rungs closer so the ladder is easier to climb.

Breaking Actions Down

State the goal you would like to achieve.

I would like to: _____

Imagine steps that would help you prepare or chip away at the goal.

The steps I can do are:

1. _____

2. _____

3. _____

4. _____

5. _____

6. _____

7. _____

8. _____

9. _____

10. _____

Imagine you are observing yourself completing each step. What would you see?

_____

_____

_____

_____

Let's break down this process even more. Choose one of the steps on your list that helps you move toward your goal. What three actions do you need to do in order to complete the step?

Step to break down into actions: _____

Action 1: _____

How often do you need to do it? Circle days of the week:

Sun   Mon   Tues   Wed   Thurs   Fri   Sat

How many hours would your action take on those days? _____

What resources do you have to achieve this action? Your resources are: _____

_____

_____

_____

Who might be able to help you with this action? People who may help are: _____

_____

_____

What do you think might be the result of completing this action? The result you anticipate is:

_____

_____

_____

_____

_____

Action 2: _____

How often do you need to do it? Circle days of the week:

Sun   Mon   Tues   Wed   Thurs   Fri   Sat

How many hours would your action take on those days? _____

What resources do you have to achieve this action? Your resources are: _____

_____

_____

_____

Who might be able to help you with this action? People who may help are: _____

_____

_____

What do you think might be the result of completing this action? The result you anticipate is:

_____

_____

_____

_____

_____

Action 3: _____

How often do you need to do it? Circle days of the week:

Sun   Mon   Tues   Wed   Thurs   Fri   Sat

How many hours would your action take on those days? _____

What resources do you have to achieve this action? Your resources are: _____

_____

_____

_____

Who might be able to help you with this action? People who may help are: _____

_____

_____

What do you think might be the result of completing this action? The result you anticipate is:

_____

_____

_____

_____

_____

By answering these questions, Sandy concludes that she really does want to go to a meeting, and she wants to know more about meetings in the community before she commits to attending. She decides that, for her, it will be important to gather more information first. She wants to research various 12-step meetings and has decided to explore other non-12-step support groups such as a Cannabis Quitters' group at a nearby mental health clinic and LifeRing Secular Recovery. The steps she will take will include gathering data on the meeting times and structures by looking at their websites and reading online articles. She will search "recovery meetings" in a private browser that does not collect her data, and she will make sure to read the philosophy of each meeting. Sandy doesn't use spreadsheets, but she likes putting things she finds in files. She opens a Word document and writes a one-sentence summary of each program so she can keep them straight. Sandy does not have a lot of time, but with this search and cut-and-paste process, she knows she can locate about one to two groups during an afternoon break. She feels confident that in a week, she will have about a dozen different programs she can explore.

As we complete this chapter, go back and reread your collected change talk. What do you notice about what you wrote? Are there any dominant themes?

_____

_____

_____

_____

_____

_____

Does your exploration of change talk bring up any emotions or automatic thoughts?

_____

_____

_____

_____

Write any additional self-reflection about the change talk:

_____

_____

_____

_____

_____

_____

_____

_____

_____

_____

_____

Consider what the themes, thoughts, and emotions say about your change process. Quite often having some sense of the overall feel of the change talk can help guide your first movement toward change. Having explored change, in the next chapter we will address how you might use micro-skills associated with MI to deepen and strengthen your own conversations about and actions toward change.

CHAPTER 10

Plan for Your Future

You have come a long way on your journey of self-discovery regarding your relationship to substances. It is likely that you have identified some ideas for using your new insights to promote change. Now is the time to pull together all that you have learned about yourself over the course of completing this workbook. To move toward creating meaningful and useful next steps, we'll use the summary skill. This is a useful tool of motivational interviewing that allows you to collect your change talk. By using the summary skill, you can be organized and prepared to take the next steps to create your own personal change plan.

Collect a Bouquet of Themes

Ever wonder why you don't usually find single flowers at the florist? The simplest answer is that it would not be profitable to sell a single flower, so it makes sense that flowers are sold in bouquets. Although we can buy single flowers, we rarely do. Bouquets are much more beautiful because they either bring together many flowers that are nearly identical or a variety of blooms in a diversity of colors and textures, resulting in an artistic statement. Even if we do not have words to describe it, the aesthetic beauty of a well-constructed bouquet inspires awe and demands our attention.

Motivational interviewing uses the bouquet metaphor as a way to describe how a summary of themes can come together vividly (Miller and Rollnick 2023). A *summary intervention* is a collection of the themes we have been exploring in your exercise answers so far. Bringing them together can help you focus on what you have decided is important. Like a floral bouquet, the verbal or written summary makes an impression. It catches your attention. By bringing together a number of themes, the summary helps you see a path forward. It can bring a dilemma into focus, be a bridge between ideas you are considering, or help organize you so you can prepare for your next steps.

For all these reasons, summary can be an especially helpful tool as you explore your relationship to substances. If you have completed even a few of the prior chapters of this workbook, you have likely come up with some themes regarding your use of substances. Maybe you even have some statements reflecting change talk: desire, ability, reason, need, commitment, intention, or steps toward change. The summary can be your tool to help organize all this hard-earned thinking, which can, in turn, inspire a next step.

Practice Summarizing

Summarizing pulls together the themes in your ideas about change. It helps you work with the thoughts we are exploring, but it can take a bit of practice to do skillfully. Start by listening for, identifying, and labeling the dominant themes in the following story.

★ Renee's Story

Renee has been using cannabis since she was a teen. Now fifty-eight, she is thinking about the next phase of her life. Renee wants to retire in four years, and she is reflecting carefully on how she wants to spend her retirement years. Although she likes cannabis—she likes to "check out and not think of anything important" when she smokes—she is concerned about the amount of money she spends on smokable and edible cannabis products. She also doesn't like seeing her nephew use cannabis, and she is increasingly concerned that she is not being a good role model for him. She wants more information on what type of life plan will work best for her.

What are some dominant themes in Renee's story? By identifying and writing down the ideas and concerns that are the most important to her, you are practicing careful listening and prioritizing the behaviors she is most likely to want to change in her life. When you practice this skill, you increase your ability to identify the most important themes for focus in your own life. Try to list at least three or four.

_____

_____

_____

_____

_____

Now, take Renee's dominant themes and create a paragraph that links the themes. It does not have to be perfect. Imagine that you are cutting the flowers and placing them in a vase. Just notice how the themes come together.

_____

_____

_____

_____

There are many possible ways to create a summary based on what you identified as Renee's dominant themes. Here is a possible summary for Renee and it is provided as an example of what a summary can be like. You might notice that yours is quite similar or a bit different. While each summary provides a slightly different focus, it still works to help clarify what is important to Renee.

"Renee has been using cannabis for much of her life, and she notices that she is entering a new phase of life, which has her rethinking smoking weed. Although she appreciates being able to 'check out,' she wants to save money for retirement and she values being a good role model for her nephew."

Do you notice that the word "but" is not used in this summary? The word "and" is used between sentences. Using "and" instead of "but" is important. When you consider that you want to keep smoking, but you also would like to quit, the "but" creates two sides. This might make you feel that you have to defend one side or the other. When "and" is used instead, it shows that two things can be true at the same time: You can both really want to keep smoking while you also very much want to quit. It is the tension between these two desires that will eventually help move you toward resolving your discomfort with the current state of things—the "status quo."

Summarizing Your Story

Pulling together some of your thoughts from the exercises you completed earlier in the book can help provide focus and clarity on your next steps in the change process. Return to chapter 5 and review your various reflections. Do you notice any dominant themes among the paraphrases, continuations of paragraphs, metaphors, double-sided reflections, or reflections of feelings? You might quickly notice that some themes are rather obvious—or you might not notice any clear themes at all. If no clear themes emerge, reread your answers in chapter 5 and list the reflections that impact you the most right now. It is quite likely these reflections are important to you even if their immediate meaning is not obvious.

Your dominant themes in the chapter 5 reflection exercises:

_____

_____

_____

_____

_____

_____

Now that you have some dominant themes, how might you pull them together in a paragraph? Write the paragraph here:

_____

_____

_____

_____

Reread the paragraph. How does having a summary of your dominant themes shape your understanding of your relationship to substances?

_____

_____

_____

_____

How does summarizing shift your focus regarding your relationship to substances? As an example, Renee wrote: "I can see that I am becoming a new person as I get older. Cannabis seems like something I used to do to cope, but now I have different responsibilities such as making sure I can take care of myself and being present and available for my nephew."

_____

_____

_____

_____

Summarizing Your Strengths

Similarly, bringing together all of your strengths can help you focus on the most powerful and effective aspects of your character. Review your answers to the exercises in chapter 6 where you identified and affirmed many of your strengths. Reread your answers. What themes emerge? If you are not identifying any themes, what specific affirmations are the most meaningful and impactful when you read them again? You might want to consider reading the affirmations out loud as they may be more meaningful when you hear yourself state your strengths.

What are the dominant themes as you explored your strengths in chapter 6?

_____

_____

_____

_____

_____

Create a paragraph that summarizes these strengths:

_____

_____

_____

_____

_____

_____

Now reread your strengths summary. What emerges for you in terms of how you see yourself?

_____

_____

_____

How might understanding yourself as a person with these strengths help you approach the next steps in exploring your relationship to alcohol and drugs?

_____

_____

_____

_____

_____

_____

Your Change Talk Summary

Return to chapter 8 and notice all the change talk that emerged from the evocative questions in the section titled "What Is Your Relationship to Substances?" Write summaries using three to four answers for each question. See Renee's example for ideas. Perfection is not important.

Renee reviewed her answers to the questions and noticed that addressing her cannabis use is very important to her (a 7 out of 10 rating). She was able to see that it is so important to her because she strongly values her relationship with her nephew. She views her relationship with him as more of a parental relationship because she does not have children and the rest of their family live out of state. This makes her an important family member in his life.

Renee also sees that she has a vision of herself being more physically active in retirement than she currently is. She hopes that with less time sitting at a desk, she can be out in the community with her dog and her friends. Saving money is also an important priority for Renee and a significant reason for stopping her use. She is aware that being on a fixed income will be limiting, and she wants as much freedom as possible as she focuses on what she enjoys in life and moves away from things that are not meaningful or engaging to her.

As she dreams of how she will move throughout her day with her dog and friends in retirement, she feels calmer and much joy. This sense of calm inspires the thought that she will not need to use as much cannabis. Renee wrote that a reason for quitting is to reduce the cravings she experiences when she goes for a day or two without smoking.

Renee strongly connects with all of these aspects of a future without cannabis. She also wrote in her change chapter that she knows stopping cannabis would not be easy, but she was able to quit when she had to submit to drug tests at a former job, and she knows she is capable of not smoking.

When bringing together all of these reasons and desires for change, Renee created this summary paragraph:

Although I know not smoking cannabis will be difficult, I see myself having a life that is free from it. I see myself spending time with my friends and dog in the community away from the office. I am no longer trapped inside. I will be able to spend time with my nephew, and I will not have to be worried that I am showing him how to cope with weed. He will make his own choices about whether or not he uses cannabis; I want him to make his choices without being concerned that I am influencing him too much.

Now it's your turn. What are the dominant themes in the change talk you identified in chapter 8?

_____

_____

_____

_____

_____

Create a paragraph that summarizes these themes:

_____

_____

_____

_____

_____

When you are done, reread all of your summaries. Taken together, notice how you are feeling or thinking about your substance use as a result. Write down those feelings and thoughts.

_____

_____

_____

_____

_____

Collecting our change talk allows us to potentially make the next step in exploring our relationship to substances. Specifically, consider your own change talk summaries. Circle or highlight one of the summaries that might be especially relevant to your exploration of your relationship to substances.

Your Summaries

Similar to Renee, you might find it useful to acknowledge your current state of affairs and then add your own reasons, needs, desires, and abilities to your own change summaries. Include any steps or commitments toward change that you have already made.

As with previous sections, review your change talk exploration in chapter 9. List four of the most relevant dominant change themes that came up in those exercises.

_____

_____

_____

_____

Using these dominant themes, write your change summary here:

_____

_____

_____

Reread your change summary. How does hearing your change summary impact any change you might want to make in relationship to your substance use?

_____

_____

_____

_____

If you find it helpful, you can always go back and explore your answers in the prior paragraphs. Perhaps you would like to do that before you begin the final chapter—you're almost there!—where we review all that you have learned about yourself and what your possible next steps in exploring your relationship to substances might be.

As you responded to the questions in this chapter, you might have noticed the power that lies in bringing together and summarizing your dominant themes. It can be helpful to develop a practice of pulling together various ideas or experiences and then asking yourself, *What next?*

Briefly reflect on where you might like to go next in your life. In what way does organizing your thinking help you take the next step in moving in that direction?

_____

_____

_____

_____

_____

_____

Notice that you are considering where you might *want* to go instead of rigidly sticking to a direction or outcome. You can always move toward something—for example, exploring a program, process, or idea—and then recognize that perhaps that is *not* what you want to do next. Learning from where you start to explore is part of a change process, and you do not need to feel compelled to stick to it if it is not working for you.

Now that you have collected your thoughts, you can move on to the next step of planning your change. Let's look now at creating SMART and CLEAR goals. Both SMART and CLEAR goals help shape and focus our desired goals in ways that we are much more likely to complete. You do not have to do both SMART and CLEAR goals. Both formats are provided here so you can choose which one you prefer when creating your change plan.

SMART and CLEAR Goals

Motivational interviewing helps you explore change based on your own personal motivation. This results in goal setting that guides your change process (Miller and Rollnick 2023). A change plan that lays out the specific steps is a common format to help guide you to where you want to go.

SMART Goals

SMART goals can help you build a change plan, as they help you obtain clarity on what and how something is being done. Knowing how to get started on a goal is especially important when changing substance use behaviors. If you decide to quit smoking cigarettes, it is good to know if you are completely stopping all cigarettes, for how long, and if it can be done the way you have planned. Although there are some variations on what each letter represents, the SMART acronym typically represents:

S - Specific

M - Measurable

A - Attainable

R - Relevant

T - Time bound

A SMART goal is one that is *specific*—you know what exactly you are supposed to be doing. It is *measurable*, that is, you know when it will be done because you can measure the amount of change. *Attainable* refers to your ability to complete the goal. If something is important and meaningful to you, it will be *relevant*. When it is *time bound*, it provides you with a time frame for when to start and when to finish. All these factors help you create a goal that you feel you can start.

Jimmi *specifically* wants to cut down on smoking cigarettes. His goal might be to cut down from twenty to ten cigarettes each day, which is *measurable*. The goal is *attainable* in that, although it will be a challenge for Jimmi, he has support to do it. It is *relevant* because cutting back on smoking is affecting his health, and that is something he cares about. Finally, he has a *time-bound* expectation: he is going to cut back to ten cigarettes for three weeks. After three weeks, maybe Jimmi will reassess his smoking. For instance, he might choose to continue to cut down—this time from ten to five cigarettes per day.

SMART is a helpful format when your goals are clear. The challenge with SMART goals emerges when you do not have a specific goal or if you are unsure about the goal, but you would like to move in some direction.

CLEAR Goals

For you, finding a goal-setting process that is especially relevant to a harm-reduction approach may be important. You might find that the CLEAR goal format enables you to more easily, flexibly, and usefully alter your movement toward change (Kreek 2020). These goals are:

C - Collaborative

L - Limited

E - Emotional

A - Appreciable

R - Refinable

Let's take a closer look at each characteristic of a CLEAR goal.

Collaborative: In this workbook, you are creating your own goals for change. But in many settings, professional helpers or guides often lead the process of goal formation. At least part of the reason these goals are not achieved is that you had little say in what the final goal would be. Given that you are working on your own change plan here, you have complete freedom to create your own change target. Although such freedom is important, you might still want to check in with someone whose opinion you trust. You might even want to refer back to chapter 7 to remind yourself of who you have in your corner and what resources you might check out in order to plan your change goal.

Jimmi was frustrated that he couldn't cut down from a pack to half a pack of cigarettes per day. He seriously doubted whether or not he could even quit smoking. Several times he tried to quit "cold turkey," but he couldn't last a day without a cigarette. Jimmi wanted to give up on the whole thing, but his change talk reminded him of his difficulty with asthma and bronchitis. His father had died of emphysema, and he did not want his children to go through the same preventable loss. Jimmi's sister, Sarah, asked how his cutting back was going, and he told her he had given in. According to Jimmi, he had to cut back significantly or totally quit smoking. He did not see any other options. Sarah quit smoking herself seven years earlier, so she had a lot of ideas about different ways Jimmi could think through some other options. Jimmi trusted Sarah, and he knew he could tell her if he did not like an idea she might share. He agreed to listen to some of her ideas, and he liked starting off with not immediately quitting, but making a first step—like going to a drop-in smoking-cessation information session. Now that he had some other options, he felt more hopeful, and he was pleased to have Sarah for support.

Limited: You might find yourself overwhelmed with starting a change project if it seems there is no clear end in sight. Having some sense of committing to working on a project for a limited amount of time can help you connect to feeling that your chosen task can be achieved. If you don't know when something will end, you may lose interest and give up.

Jimmi knows he can go to a smoking-cessation information and support group and attend up to eight sessions. He likes knowing that he has some time to think through what he might do next, and he is also relieved that he is not committing to being in a group forever. Jimmi would feel more compelled to take a step toward his next action when the group meetings ended after eight sessions. The expectation he had for himself was to act on his new knowledge and trust the support he'd received in the group sessions.

Emotional: According to the developers of the CLEAR acronym, having an emotional connection to the goal is critical. Our motivation to change is typically fueled by an emotional connection to people, places, and things that are important to us (Kreek 2020). Changing behavior, thoughts, and attitudes takes time and energy. If you do not have an emotional connection to the change—that is, if it is not important to you—moving toward the goal can become a chore. However, with an emotional connection you are more likely to prioritize the work that needs to be done to complete the necessary tasks.

Jimmi had a strong emotional connection to his change goal—cutting down or quitting smoking. He felt defeated by not being able to quit smoking or cut down, and he had significant motivation because he had so much love for his children; he did not want them to experience what he went through when he lost his father at a young age. He also noticed his change talk felt emotional when he read it on the page—all the reasons he needed to quit so he could be present for his children and the benefits that could come if he stopped smoking so much. He also noticed in his change talk how passionate he was about being willing to participate in a group and being open to hear about ideas on how to finally quit smoking.

Appreciable: Although this is not a commonly used term, "appreciable" refers to our ability to break down the goal into smaller steps. Smaller steps are almost always useful because you build confidence and increase hope each time you complete another step. In fact, all goals are typically a series of smaller steps. Clearly identifying how a goal will be broken down allows you to think about how the smaller steps will occur. Without thinking about the smaller steps, you may feel overwhelmed.

> Jimmi liked the idea that the smoking-cessation group would help him get some ideas, and he would also be able to connect with others who could relate and offer support. Jimmi was glad the group had a beginning and an end date. He had specific days he planned to attend each week, and knew that over time he would be building more knowledge and support for managing the physical and emotional aspects of quitting. He saw each week as another building block toward his goal. Together, all this would help him identify where he was the most stuck when it came to quitting smoking and where he had the most opportunity to grow and learn.

Refinable: Because your goal is "refinable," you can adjust or tweak your goal as you try it out. While we can predict what our goals might be and how we will get there, our path to change is rarely what we expect. In fact, more often than not the path to change has many twists and turns. You might start working toward a goal and then find yourself moving in a very different direction. You might even discover that what you thought was your intended change goal is actually something quite different.

> When Jimmi started the smoking-cessation group, he was eager to participate and learn. He particularly wanted to know more about options to change and various steps he could take along the path to change. What he did not expect was learning about medication-assisted treatment for nicotine addiction. Jimmi did not know there were approved medications that could help him manage withdrawal and cravings for nicotine. Once he learned about this option, Jimmi immediately knew that he wanted to talk to a doctor about medication that might help him quit smoking. He received a medical referral from the group leader, and immediately made an appointment with a doctor. Jimmi continued to attend the group sessions, but now he focused on working with his doctor to find and take medications to help him manage the physical withdrawal from nicotine.

Your CLEAR Plan

You now know quite a lot about yourself from summarizing your strengths and change talk. Looking back at your summaries, what might you do next? In this table, you have an opportunity to think about your next steps toward change. You have a lot of freedom in how you create your CLEAR plan, and as the "R" indicates, you can always adjust it as you want and need to. Jimmi's plan is in the first field. Add your plan next to his.

An area of my life I would like to change is:

_____

Collaborate Who can help me think about this change	My sister, Sarah.	
Limited How long will I need for this? When will I know it is done?	By the end of eight weeks of group, I should have a plan.	
Emotional How and why is this important to me?	I want to be alive for my kids. I don't want them to see me get sick.	
Appreciable What are some small steps?	I just need to get to group once a week.	
Refinable How might the goal shift?	I might learn sooner than eight weeks some options to help me quit smoking.	

You can make a CLEAR plan for a number of goals in your life. You might even find it useful to practice with CLEAR plans so you can see how it works for you to shift around your goals and ideas over time. A CLEAR plan offers you a lot of flexibility to move toward change. Even though the CLEAR plan can be a helpful and effective tool, you might still notice that your confidence to change is not where you want it to be. In the concluding chapter, you will be invited to try out the smallest change and learn how to get started while growing your confidence.

Taking Small Steps to Boost Your Confidence

You did it! Here you are at the end of the workbook. You have had an opportunity to look at your ability or willingness to accept yourself. You explored how to develop self-compassion and noticed your strengths. You spent some time practicing how to reflect on your own experiences and to ask yourself the big questions. You might have ended up being able to put everything together and create a plan that feels right for you, and you are ready to take the next step—or not. It is equally likely that you are here at the end of the book and are not exactly sure what to do next.

Reflecting on Your Experiences with This Book

If you find yourself less than enthusiastic, confident, or ready to take the next step, that is normal, and it is just fine. This is an excellent place to pause and do a bit of self-assessment. Spend a moment reflecting on your experiences reading the text, thinking about the stories you read, and completing the exercises. If you had to pick the top three lessons you learned from reading the book and practicing the skills, what would those lessons be?

The top three things that I learned about myself as the result of reading this book:

1. _____

2. _____

3. _____

This is a good place to start because those things that come to mind the most readily might be those things you are most able to use for your next steps. They might be particularly useful for you because they are especially important or relevant to your current situation.

You are also likely to have noticed that some ideas or practices did not fit you so well. These are newer concepts for you, or you might not feel as comfortable taking on some of these new ways of being or doing things. Any reluctance you might have to change is perfectly normal. It should be expected that you have mixed feelings about making the next steps to address your relationship with substances.

As we discussed earlier, substances can be helpful until they start to get in the way of other important priorities in our life. Because we have found ways to benefit from the substances and we might even have physical withdrawal or other discomfort if we were to give them up, it is hard to let go of them.

Given that you might not be totally comfortable with making any changes, name three ideas or practices in this book that you have difficulty bringing into your life:

1. _____

2. _____

3. _____

Compare your two lists. Are there items on the first list that would help you address your concerns on the second list? It is possible that the lists are somehow related. Because of that, we may be able to start where we have some comfort and use that comfort to approach the places where we feel less sure about ourselves and our needs.

★ Lucy's Story

Lucy had been using cocaine with friends since high school. She is twenty-seven now. She picked up this book because she had a friend who stopped using cocaine socially as he was worried about how much money he was spending on it. He told Lucy that he was also worried about having serious health issues as cocaine is increasingly cut with synthetic opioids such as fentanyl, and he was anxious about overdose risk and possibly becoming addicted to opioids. Lucy became concerned when she spoke with her friend, but she had mixed feelings about giving up cocaine. She very much enjoyed using the drug to party with friends on the weekends, and she had also heard about people overdosing from cocaine when it is cut with other substances.

Lucy learned about herself in the process of reading this book. At this point in the journey, Lucy realized that she remains somewhat uncomfortable noticing what cocaine does for her, aside from allowing her to have fun with friends. She does feel badly about her use, and she worries that she might be holding herself back from other possible goals and life experiences. She also did not connect to the idea of self-compassion, because more often than not she labels herself a "loser," and she gets frustrated with how she has not been able to stop using cocaine.

After reading both of her lists, Lucy thinks, *I am both surprised and not surprised.* She noticed that her new awareness of her strengths revealed how she was judging and punishing herself for using cocaine. She even noticed saying to herself, *I guess I have a lot more shame than I realized.*

Now, review both of your lists. If it is helpful, rewrite the lists here, so you can see them side by side:

What I Learned	Ideas or Activities That Are Still Difficult for Me

You have an amazing brain that can help you see relationships between things that, at first, you might think are unrelated (Hayes 2019). In this book, we have summarized skills and attitudes associated with motivational interviewing, which are supported by decades of research (Miller and Moyers 2021). It is quite likely that the skills or concepts you connect with on the left can be used to help you develop confidence in dealing with the ideas and concepts on the right. Lucy can provide us with an additional example.

Lucy feels confident about her ability to notice things about herself and reflect on how she is feeling and thinking in various situations. She had experience as a teenager being part of a journaling club, and throughout her life she has enjoyed writing in diaries. She realized she could continue to write down thoughts about herself and practice noticing what she was saying about herself instead of ignoring it. Maybe that could lead to becoming more open to and accepting of her own story. She also thought that maybe she could practice the self-compassion exercises in her journaling.

Lucy continues to be uncertain about her cocaine use, but she is becoming increasingly open to exploring the impact of her drug use. She no longer pushes it away or ignores it. She also notices that, as she begins to accept where she is even just a bit more, she catches herself thinking and writing about more reasons to change. Slowly, Lucy is beginning to feel less shame and more confident about her first steps toward changing her life by changing her relationship with cocaine.

Given Lucy's experience, you might also start to notice how you can use your confidence and abilities to change to move forward. Review your two lists again. In what way might using your skills and understanding in the left column help you work on the ideas and behaviors in the right column? The good news is you only need one idea that you can use to get started on a plan to make a change in your life around your substance use.

_____

_____

You might feel confident practicing the skills in this book, and the last question might have helped you consider where to take the first steps toward change. It is also possible that you still may not have an idea of what your next step might be. If you remain unclear about your next step or you want to help any action you take be quick and uncomplicated, consider making a brief action plan for yourself.

Getting the Ball Rolling When You Feel Stuck

In *brief action planning*, we find one action we are willing to do, and feel confident about doing, in a specific period of time (Gutnick et al. 2014). Brief action planning helps us to get the ball rolling when we are considering change, but do not know exactly how to do that. It also helps when we are not able to commit to a larger or more long-term goal. This method makes sense in almost any situation because almost all changes we care about require us to make many little changes in order to get to our ultimate end point. Remember from the last chapter, CLEAR goals involve making our goals "appreciable"—that is, breaking them down into smaller goals or steps.

The first question to ask yourself regarding a brief action plan is this: *Is there anything I would like to work on in the coming weeks?* In a couple of words or sentences, write your response here (Gutnick et al. 2014):

_____

_____

_____

_____

_____

_____

Consider the action you are thinking about taking. What are the who, what, where, when, and how of your action? This builds on the SMART or CLEAR goals you set in chapter 10.

Who: _____

What: _____

Where: _____

When: _____

How: _____

Now that you have some idea of what you would like to do and how it might be done, how confident are you that you would be able to achieve this goal given your plans? Choose a number between 1 and 10 (1 = not being confident at all and 10 = being very confident).

Not Confident					Confident				Very Confident	
1	2	3	4	5	6	7	8	9	1	0

Is your response a 7 or above? If so, it appears you have enough confidence to give it a go. If you are a 6 or less, what would need to happen for your score to move up to a 7?

_____

_____

_____

_____

_____

Once you are at a 7 or above in confidence about getting started, think about who you would like to check in with (if anyone) about your change. When would you like to talk to them? Checking in with someone is important in making even small steps work as it keeps you accountable to someone for your behavior. Think about people you know who post to social media when they are starting a new goal or making a change. Being public with your change plan is a way to build support, and it keeps you "honest" about whether or not you have been trying to make the change.

Someone who can help support my change plan: _____

A couple of months after Lucy noticed her lack of acceptance and self-compassion, she thought she might be ready to make a change regarding how and when she used cocaine. Lucy's self-exploration work allowed her to recognize that on the mornings after she used, she was especially listless and irritable. She did not like snapping at her friend or partner, and realizing this pattern, she came up with a brief action plan that made sense in a CLEAR goal framework. Lucy's CLEAR goal looked like this:

Collaborative: The goal was Lucy's idea, but she did check with a good friend and her sister to make sure it sounded realistic. She liked having others know what she was doing so she could have people support her and hold her accountable.

Limited: Lucy decided she wanted to try cutting back on cocaine for the next six months. She would reevaluate her use after the six months ended.

Emotional: Lucy recognized how much she cared about how she treated people when she finished the exercises in this workbook. She felt committed to change.

Appreciable: Lucy planned to break down her goals into monthly brief action goals, so the overall change did not feel so overwhelming.

Refinable: Lucy understood that she could review her progress and decide if she needed to be less ambitious in her cocaine reduction or if she could cut back even more after reducing her use for a month or two.

Lucy's brief action plan was to not use cocaine on Friday nights for a full month. She found this to be a reasonable and limited goal as she could see how it felt. She might be able to break down or alter the goal—for example, maybe she would change the date to a Saturday or even try not using on both days. This goal was emotional for her as it gave her hope and increased her self-respect. Lucy chose this goal for herself rather than someone else choosing it for her, so it is more meaningful for Lucy and supports her autonomy.

Rating her confidence was a challenge for Lucy. She gave herself a 4 regarding her confidence in cutting back to one day per party weekend. When considering what would help her rise to a 7 in confidence, Lucy recognized that she has friends who make it very hard for her to say no to cocaine. They offer it to her and always speak about how much they look forward to being together to "party." It was not easy for Lucy, but she realized there was no way she would be successful if she was at a party with these friends—at least not now. Lucy knows one of her values is honesty, and she did not want to lie to her friends by making up excuses regarding why she was not showing up at parties. She decided she would be best served if she talked to her friends before any party weekend to let them know she was cutting back and would not be present for all the events. By calling her friends in advance, Lucy felt more confident in her ability to step away from using for the short term, and her confidence rating increased to a 7.

Lucy thought about whether she wanted to check in with someone about her progress. She did not want to check in with her friends, as it might feel awkward if she is cutting back and many of her friends are still using cocaine. She decided to check in with one of her sisters. Her sister knows that Lucy uses cocaine, but she is nonjudgmental and supportive. Lucy spoke with her sister before she started her plan, and they decided together that Lucy would call her sister once a week to check in so they could have a conversation about how Lucy was able or not able to achieve her goal that week.

Exercise: Your Own Brief Action Plan

In the table, write your steps for two brief action plans that you could take toward change. Remember, the steps you take can be very tiny. All larger change builds on small changes. You can download the exercise at http://www.newharbinger.com/51901.

My Brief Action	Example	Action 1	Action 2
What's the plan (who, what, where, when, how)?	Smoke less. Cut back from 5 bowls of weed a day to 3 bowls.		
What is my confidence from 1 to 10?	5		
If 6 or below, what can I do to reach a 7?	Get rid of the cannabis in my house. Give my pipes to my friend.		
Once I am a 7, with whom and when do I check in about my progress?	Talk to my therapist weekly. Let her know I am doing this.		

Return to this question after the designated time has passed. If you succeeded in reaching your goal from your first brief action plan, congratulations! How does that feel?

_____

_____

_____

_____

It is likely you might feel good or great, and you may be very ready to move on to your next action step. Even if you do not feel completely wonderful as the result of achieving a small goal, making small changes supports the effort you have made, and it helps build your confidence in your ability to follow through on goals and create a more meaningful life.

What if you did not achieve your goal or achieved only part of a goal? You might remember from chapter 3 that we do not fail, we FAIL (First Attempt In Learning). If you find that you did not achieve a goal, you have an opportunity to notice what needs to be adjusted in order to succeed. It is quite possible that your first goal was not exactly doable in the time you hoped to achieve it. This is fine, and this often happens! CLEAR goals can always be further broken down into smaller steps. In the example, maybe cutting back from five bowls a week to three is too difficult. If so, it's time to reevaluate this goal. To start, it might make sense to cut back to four bowls per week. You can always give yourself the gift of time. Who says that a change has to occur within a week or two? Break it down and give yourself more time to make the change. Similar to testing out recipes in the kitchen, the recipes for life might also need adjustment in order to succeed.

Identify some smaller steps you can do if the first goal is too much to achieve right now.

_____

_____

_____

Your timing window for taking these steps is: _____

Congratulations on finishing this exploration process! Hopefully you learned about yourself in ways that you found interesting, enjoyable, and valuable. The path to change and growth in life is never a straight line. Once you realize that you have your own sweet and challenging path to follow, you might find yourself enjoying the unique journey that builds on your next steps. Considering all you have learned and will continue to learn and explore, find a place to take your first step, which may be the small step that leads you to the next chapter of your life.

Acknowledgments

Deepest gratitude to Ann-Marie Murphy. You not only pestered me to write for twenty years (thank you!), but you also provided the inspiration for all that is on these pages. You are the embodiment of all that is compassionate and engaged care, and I have learned so much about how to be a good human from you.

To Adam, Mr. Dr. Dempsey, for never giving up on me or anyone. You give hope and dignity to so many, and we love you for your brilliance and presence. I could not be more grateful for your love and support.

To all you help seekers who allowed me to support you on your journey. Some of you got the early version and were patient with my learning. Others got the later version, and you were kind to me as well. You all have taught me so much about survival, determination, and the power of hope and trust to light the way.

To my patient and persistent editors at New Harbinger: Ryan Buresh, Jennifer Holder, and Jean Blomquist. Your thoughtful editing and respect for the project helped to transform this book and I learned so much from your guidance and wisdom.

Resources

To support learning about yourself and your substance use, here are a few websites and numbers that can help you explore the private and discreet services offered by community agencies.

LifeRing Recovery

https://lifering.org

1-800-811-4142

LifeRing Recovery promotes itself as a secular, sobriety-oriented, self-help organization. Similar to 12-step, it is not facilitated by professionals but rather by peers. LifeRing provides peer groups that share coping skills, and it states that it promotes flexibility by encouraging individuals to engage with whatever recovery supports work for them.

National Institute on Alcohol Abuse and Alcoholism

https://www.niaaa.nih.gov

301-443-3860

NIAAA is a comprehensive resource on current education and research addressing alcohol use and its impacts.

National Institute on Drug Abuse

https://nida.nih.gov

301-443-6441

NIDA offers extensive information on drug abuse, based on the most recent research.

NEXT Social Support Guide

https://nextdistro.org/socialsupport#online

NEXT is a harm-reduction organization dedicated to linking individuals to harm reduction resources that meet specific substance use exploration needs. This list includes moderation and well as abstinence-based groups and online groups for people using substances as well as friends of people using substances.

Substance Abuse and Mental Health Services Administration National Helpline

https://www.samhsa.gov/find-help/national-helpline

1-800-662-HELP (4357)

Operated 24/7, the SAMHSA National Helpline provides information and referrals if you or a loved one are facing mental health or substance use issues. The confidential service does not provide counseling, but it can direct you to helpful resources, treatment facilities, and support groups in your area.

Secular Organization for Sobriety

https://www.sossobriety.org

314-353-3532

The SOS is a network of autonomous and secular peer-run recovery groups that address alcohol, food, and drug use disorders. SOS support groups enable members to share stories and coping skills. The emphasis is on skills for relapse prevention with no connection to religious or spiritual practices.

12-Step Versions in Different Fellowships

https://12step.org/references/12-step-versions

12-step is used by millions of people as its philosophy has been adapted to many substance use and behavioral concerns. The fellowships in this list follow the process of 12-step group meetings. It describes how different groups use variations of the 12-step process. You can go to 12-step meetings to check out the program and meet people who are involved in their own process of dealing with their relationship to substances. If you are not committed to changing your relationship to substances, you may find attending 12-step programs challenging as they are designed to ultimately support abstaining from all substance use.

References

American Psychiatric Association. 2022. *Diagnostic and Statistical Manual of Mental Disorders.* 5th ed., text revision. Washington, DC: American Psychiatric Association Publishing.

Arnold, K. 2014. "Behind the Mirror: Reflective Listening and Its Tain in the Work of Carl Rogers." *The Humanistic Psychologist* 42(4): 354–369.

Bustamante, J. 2023. "NCDAS: Substance Abuse and Addiction Statistics." *NCDAS*, January. drugabusestatistics.org.

de Almeida Neto, A. 2017. "Understanding Motivational Interviewing: An Evolutionary Perspective." *Evolutionary Psychological Science* 3(4): 379–389.

Gutnick, D., K. Reims, C. Davis, H. Gainforth, M. Jay, and S. Cole. 2014. "Brief Action Planning to Facilitate Behavior Change and Support Patient Self-Management." *Journal of Outcome Management* 21: 17–29.

Harm Reduction Therapy Center. 2022. "What Is Harm Reduction Therapy?" https://harmreduction therapy.org/what-is-harm-reduction-therapy.

Harris, R. 2021. "Forty Common Values: A Checklist." https://overcoming.co.uk/_data/site/148/prod uct/533/40valueschecklist-2021.pdf.

Hayes, S. 2019. *A Liberated Mind: How to Pivot Toward What Matters.* New York: Avery.

Kreek, A. 2020. "CLEAR Goals Are Better Than SMART Goals." *Kreek Speak* (blog), February 6. https://www.kreekspeak.com/clear-goal-setting.

Linehan, M. M. 1993. *Cognitive–Behavioral Treatment of Borderline Personality Disorder.* New York: Guilford Press.

——. 2015. *DBT Skills Training Manual: Second Edition.* New York: Guilford Press.

Lynch, T. R. 2018. *Radically Open Dialectical Behavior Therapy: Theory and Practice for Treating Disorders of Overcontrol.* Oakland, CA: New Harbinger Publications.

Miller, W. R., A. A. Forcehimes, and A. Zweben. 2019. *Treating Addiction: A Guide for Professionals.* 2nd ed. New York: Guilford Press.

Miller, W. R., and T. B. Moyers. 2021. *Effective Psychotherapists: Clinical Skills That Improve Client Outcomes*. New York: Guilford Press.

Miller, W. R., and S. Rollnick. 2023. *Motivational Interviewing: Helping People Change and Grow*. 4th ed. New York: Guilford Press.

Moodian, M. 2015. "Lessons of Compassion from the Dalai Lama." July 24. https://www.huffpost.com/entry/lessons-of-compassion-fro_b_7868940.

National Institute on Alcohol Abuse and Alcoholism. 2019–2022. "Alcohol's Effects on Health." https://www.niaaa.nih.gov/publications/brochures-and-fact-sheets/alcohol-facts-and-statistics.

Neff, K. D. 2023. "Self-Compassion: Theory, Method, Research, and Intervention." *Annual Review of Psychology* 74(1): 193–218.

Rosengren, D. B. 2017. *Building Motivational Interviewing Skills: A Practitioner Workbook*. New York: Guilford Press.

Sifton, E. 2003. *The Serenity Prayer: Faith and Politics in Times of Peace and War*. New York: W. W. Norton.

Spacey, J. 2021. "160 Examples of Attitudes." *Simplicable*, January 12. https://simplicable.com/society/attitudes.

———. 2021. "206 Examples of Strengths." *Simplicable*, July 15. https://simplicable.com/talent/strengths.

Kristin L. Dempsey, EdD, LMFT, LPCC, is a psychotherapist, counselor educator, and trainer. For thirty years, she has supported individuals with exploring their own relationships to substances. She is a member of the Motivational Interviewing Network of Trainers (MINT), and has been privileged to provide motivational interviewing (MI) training to thousands of people in behavioral health, primary care, public health, school, corrections, and human services organizations.

Foreword writer **Dee-Dee Stout, MA**, is a member of MINT, and a founding member of the Northern California Association of Harm Reduction Therapists & Providers. Stout has more than thirty-five years' experience in the field of addiction, and is author of *Coming to Harm Reduction Kicking and Screaming.*

MORE BOOKS from
NEW HARBINGER PUBLICATIONS

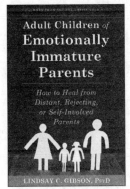
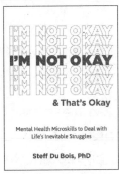
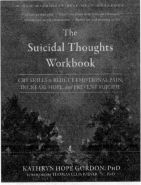

Did you know there are **free tools** you can download for this book?

Free tools are things like **worksheets**, **guided meditation exercises**, and **more** that will help you get the most out of your book.

You can download free tools for this book—whether you bought or borrowed it, in any format, from any source—from the New Harbinger website. All you need is a NewHarbinger.com account. Just use the URL provided in this book to view the free tools that are available for it. Then, click on the "download" button for the free tool you want, and follow the prompts that appear to log in to your NewHarbinger.com account and download the material.

You can also save the free tools for this book to your **Free Tools Library** so you can access them again anytime, just by logging in to your account! Just look for this button on the book's free tools page.

+ Save this to my free tools library

If you need help accessing or downloading free tools, visit **newharbinger.com/faq** or contact us at **customerservice@newharbinger.com**.